A SURE GUIDE TO HEAVEN

A Sure Guide
to Heaven

JOSEPH ALLEINE

THE BANNER OF TRUTH TRUST

THE BANNER OF TRUTH TRUST
3 Murrayfield Road, Edinburgh EH12 6EL
P.O. Box 621, Carlisle, Pennsylvania 17013, USA

∗

First published 1671
First Banner of Truth Trust reprint 1959
Paperback edition 1964
Reprinted 1967
Reprinted 1978
Reprinted 1989
ISBN 0 85151 081 7

∗

Printed and bound in Great Britain by
Hazell Watson & Viney Limited
Member of BPCC plc
Aylesbury, Bucks

Contents

Biographical introduction

Joseph Alleine was born into a Puritan family at Devizes, in Wiltshire, and baptized on April 8th, 1634. England was then in the throes of the stirring events that were soon to lead to the Civil War, and before Alleine was ten years old the Market Square, where his home stood, echoed with the crash of cannon and the peal of musket as Royalist put Roundhead to flight at the battle of Roundway (July 1643). Two years later the tables were turned and Cromwell himself saw to it that the blue banner of Parliament was raised aloft over the old castle that stood opposite the home of Alleine's childhood. The family circle was also not without its trials. His father, though a clothier of good standing, suffered some of the economic misfortunes of war; and to their grief, Joseph's eldest brother, Edward, already in the ministry, died in 1645.

That same year saw Alleine 'setting forth in the Christian race' and imploring his father that he might be educated to 'succeed his brother in the work of the ministry'. Thus, in April 1649 we find him going up to Oxford to sit at the feet of such divines as John Owen and Thomas Goodwin. In November 1651 he moved from Lincoln to Corpus Christi College – the latter, under the presidency of the saintly Dr Edward Staunton, being a more thoroughgoing Puritan seminary. Here he took his B.A. on July 6th 1653, became a tutor and subsequently chaplain to the College. Doubtless it was partly due to Alleine's influence that Henry Jessey could write in 1660: 'I think there was scarce such a place in the world as Corpus Christi, where such a multitude held forth the power of godliness, and purity of God's worship. Even an Eden it was, but now a barren wilderness.'

Alleine's years at Oxford were characterized by piety and diligent study. His warm disposition found him many friends, but if their visits interrupted his studying time 'he had no leisure to let them in, saying, "It is better that they should wonder at my rudeness than that I should lose my time; for only a few will take notice of the rudeness, but many may feel my loss of time." ' As a chaplain he laboured to evangelize country villages around Oxford and also preached to the prisoners in the gaol every fortnight. Such was his training for his future ministry. Not yet twenty-one, he had already learned to be 'infinitely and insatiably greedy for the conversion of souls and to this end he poured out his very heart in prayer and in preaching'.

It is no wonder that a worthy Puritan divine, George Newton (1602–1681), minister of St Mary Magdalen, Taunton, called Alleine to be his assistant in 1655. Taunton, a wool manufacturing town with a population of perhaps some 20,000, was a Puritan stronghold in the West Country. The spirit of the town had been clearly displayed ten years earlier when, with heroic steadfastness, it had withstood more than one desperate Royalist siege – even when half the streets had been burned down by a storm of mortars and many of the inhabitants had died of starvation! It was here, amidst the hills, meadows and orchards of Somerset, that Alleine was to spend his short but unforgettable ministry.

Immediately following the commencement of his work at Taunton, Alleine was married on October 4th, 1655, to his cousin Theodosia Alleine, a woman of singular spirituality, who left a moving account of her husband's ministry. The only 'fault' for which she chided her husband was that he did not spend more time with her, to which he would reply, 'Ah, my dear, I know thy soul is safe; but how many that are perishing have I to look after? O that I could do more for them!' Alleine's whole life was an illustration of his saying, 'Give me a Christian that counts his time more precious than gold.' When the week began he would say, 'Another week is now before us, let us spend this week for God', and each morning, 'Now let us live this one day well!' 'All the time of his health', writes his wife, 'he did rise constantly at or before four o'clock, and on the Sabbath sooner, if he did wake; he would be much troubled if he heard any smiths, or shoemakers, or such tradesmen, at work at their trades before he was in his duties with God; saying to me after, "O how this noise shames me! doth not my master deserve more than theirs?" From four till eight he spent in prayer, holy contemplation, and singing of psalms, which he much delighted in, and did daily practise alone, as well as in his family.'

Together this devoted pair laboured for souls. Theodosia Alleine kept a school for children in her home, while her husband spent five afternoons every week following up the urgent calls to the unconverted which sounded forth Sunday by Sunday from beneath the stately tower of Mary Magdalen. He kept a catalogue of the names of the inhabitants of each street and saw that all were visited and catechized. This resulted in a numerous ingathering of souls.[1] 'His supplications and his exhortations', said George Newton, 'many times were so affectionate, so full of holy zeal, life, and vigour, that they quite overcame his hearers; he melted them and sometimes dissolved the hardest hearts.' It is clear that even in an age when powerful preaching and successful evangelism were comparatively common, Alleine's ministry was outstanding in the eyes of his brethren. 'Few ages have produced more eminent preachers than Mr Joseph Alleine', declared that apostolic North Country Puritan, Oliver Heywood. And Baxter speaks of his 'great ministerial skilfulness in the public explication and application of the Scriptures – so melting, so convincing, so powerful'.

A day of grace was nearing its sunset when Alleine entered

'The Lord was pleased to bless us exceedingly in our endeavours', Theodosia Alleine wrote, 'so that many were converted in a few years, that were before strangers to God.' *Joseph Alleine*, by Charles Stanford, 1861, p. 101.

upon his ministry. Within three years Cromwell was dead. Two years more and the bells at Taunton rang merrily to welcome the homecoming of Charles II and the restoration of monarchy (1660). But the happiness in Puritan hearts was short lived. For the era when, as Philip Henry said, 'a face of godliness was upon the nation' was over and in 1662, by the infamous Act of Uniformity, 2,000 of the best ministers England ever had were cast out of their pulpits. Among the eighty-five or so ministers who suffered in this way in Somerset we find, as we might well expect, the names of George Newton and Joseph Alleine. But, though debarred from his pulpit, Alleine refused to be silenced; indeed his wife tells us how, 'laying aside all other studies because he accounted his time would be but short', he increased his preaching activity: 'I know that he hath preached fourteen times in eight days, and ten often, and six and seven ordinarily in these months.'

At length after surviving many threats Alleine received a summons on May 26th 1663; the following night he appointed to meet his people 'about one or two o'clock in the morning, to which they shewed their readiness: there was of young and old many hundreds; he preached and prayed with them about three hours'. The next day he was thrown into prison at Ilchester. After a year he was released, but only to be confronted by the rigours of the Five Mile Act and the Conventicle Act. Though now declining in health, he nevertheless resumed preaching in secret until July 10th 1666. On that evening whilst he was preaching on Psalm cxlvii 20 to a gathering in a private house, the doors were battered open and he was again taken to prison. Once more he was released, and with undiminished spiritual energy he considered what he might yet do to further the Gospel of Christ. 'Now we have one day more', he would say to his wife as he rose in the morning, 'here is one more for God, now let us live well this day, work hard for our souls, lay up much treasure in heaven this day, for we have but a few to live.' His wife tells us how, with true Puritan spirit, his thoughts turned to the possibility of missionary work in Wales or even in China. Never did the evangel of Jesus Christ burn more fervently in any English heart! But Alleine's work was done, for his physical constitution never recovered from the hardships of his confinements and his body was sinking fast. On November 17th 1668 at the age of thirty-four, God took him away from the evils yet to come, and aged George Newton stood by as his body was laid to rest in the chancel of the church which had once resounded with the 'alarm' of his calls to the unconverted.

This book embodies the substance of Alleine's message and in so doing provides a true model of Puritan evangelism. Phraseology must differ from age to age and gifts from man to man, but here, we have no hesitation in saying, are the principles which must be present in any true presentation of the Gospel. More than one great evangelist has had his views moulded by the following pages. George Whitefield, while still a student at Oxford, tells us in his Journals how Alleine's *Alarm* 'much benefited' him. Charles Haddon Spurgeon records how, when he was a child, his mother would often read a piece of Alleine's *Alarm* to them as they sat round the fire on a Sunday evening, and when brought under conviction of sin it was to this old book he turned. 'I remember', he writes, 'when I used to awake in the morning, the first thing I took up was Alleine's *Alarm*, or Baxter's *Call to the Unconverted*. Oh those books, those books! I read and devoured them. . . .' With his heart thus burning with the fire of Puritan divinity, Spurgeon was prepared to follow in the steps of Alleine and Whitefield.

Countless editions of this book have been issued since it first saw the light in 1671. Dr Calamy wrote concerning it in 1702: 'Multitudes will have cause for ever to be thankful for it. No book in the English tongue (the Bible only excepted) can equal it for the number that hath been dispersed; there have been twenty thousand sold under the title of the "Call", or "Alarm", and fifty thousand of the same under the title of the "Sure Guide to Heaven", thirty thousand of which were sold at one impression.' As a remarkable illustration of the spiritual influence of this work we may mention one example. Towards the end of the eighteenth century the minister of a Highland congregation, a man more eminent for scholarship than evangelical fervour, was approached by a Society to translate the 'Alarm' into Gaelic. The book was thus passed into his hands and finding it suitable material for the pulpit he commenced to repeat the substance of its successive chapters to his congregation. The result, it is said, 'was a widespread awakening, which long prevailed in the district of Nether Lorn'.

With the prayer that the substance of this book may again be sounded forth throughout our land and across the seas, we commend this book to the blessing of Him whose word is 'quick and powerful, and sharper than any two-edged sword'. 'All flesh is as grass, and all the glory of man as the flower of grass. The grass withereth, and the flower thereof falleth away: But the word of the Lord endureth for ever. And this is the word which by the gospel is preached unto you' (1 Pet i 24–25).

1 *August* 1959   IAIN MURRAY

A Sure Guide To Heaven

An earnest invitation to sinners to turn to God

Dearly Beloved, I gladly acknowledge myself a debtor to you, and am concerned, as I would be found a good steward of the household of God, to give to every one his portion. But the physician is most concerned for those patients whose case is most doubtful and hazardous; and the father's pity is especially turned towards his dying child. So unconverted souls call for earnest compassion and prompt diligence to pluck them as brands from the burning (Jude 23). Therefore it is to them I shall first apply myself in these pages.

But from where shall I fetch my argument? With what shall I win them? O that I could tell! I would write to them in tears, I would weep out every argument, I would empty my veins for ink, I would petition them on my knees. O how thankful should I be if they would be prevailed with to repent and turn.

How long have I laboured for you! How often would I have gathered you! This is what I have prayed for and studied for these many years, that I might bring you to God. O that I might now do it! Will you yet be entreated?

'But, O Lord, how insufficient I am for this work. Alas, with what shall I pierce the scales of Leviathan, or make the heart feel that is hard as the nether millstone? Shall I go and speak to the grave, and expect the dead will obey me and come forth? Shall I make an oration to the rocks, or declaim to the mountains, and think to move them with arguments? Shall I make the blind to see? From the beginning of the world was it not heard that a man opened the eyes of the blind (Jn ix 32). But, O Lord, Thou *canst pierce the heart of the sinner. I can only draw the bow at a venture, but do Thou direct the arrow between the joints of the harness. Slay the sin, and save the soul of the sinner that casts his eyes on these pages.'*

There is no entering into heaven but by the strait passage of the second birth; without holiness you shall never see God (Heb xii 14). Therefore give yourselves unto the Lord now. Set yourselves to seek Him now. Set up the Lord Jesus in your hearts, and set Him up in your houses. Kiss the Son (Ps ii 12) and embrace the tenders of mercy; touch His sceptre and live; for why will ye die? I do not beg for myself, but would have you happy: this is the prize I run for. My soul's desire and prayer for you is, that you may be saved (Rom x 1).

I beseech you to permit a friendly plainness and freedom with you in your deepest concern. I am not playing the orator to make a learned speech to you, nor dressing the dish with eloquence in order to please you. These lines are upon a weighty errand indeed – to convince, and convert, and save you. I am not baiting my hook with rhetoric, nor fishing for your applause, but for your souls. My work is not to please you, but to save you; nor is my business with your fancies, but with your hearts. If I have not your hearts, I have nothing. If I were to please your ears, I would sing another song. If I were to preach myself, I would steer another course. I could then tell you a smoother tale; I would make pillows for you and speak peace, for how can Ahab love this Micaiah, that always prophesies evil concerning him? (1 Kgs xxii 8). But how much better are the wounds of a friend, than the fair speeches of the harlot, who flatters with her lips, till the dart strike through the liver? (Prov vii 21–23 and vi 26). If I were to quiet a crying infant, I might sing him into a happier mood, or rock him asleep; but when the child is fallen into the fire, the parent takes another course; he will not try to still him with a song or trifle. I know, if we succeed not with you, you are lost; if we cannot get your consent to arise and come away, you will perish for ever. No conversion – no salvation! I must get your good-will, or leave you miserable.

But here the difficulty of my work again occurs to me. '*O Lord, choose my stones out of the brook (1 Sam xvii 40, 45). I come in the name of the Lord of hosts, the God of the armies of Israel. I come forth, like the stripling David against Goliath, to wrestle, not with flesh and blood, but with principalities and powers, and rulers of the darkness of this world (Eph vi 12). This day let the Lord smite the Philistines, spoil the strong man of his armour, and give me the captives out of his hand. Lord, choose my words, choose my weapons for me; and when I put my hand into the bag, and take out a stone and sling it, do Thou carry it to the mark, and make it sink, not into the forehead, but into the heart of the unconverted sinner, and smite him to the ground like Saul of Tarsus (Acts ix 4).*'

Some of you do not know what I mean by conversion, and in vain shall I attempt to persuade you to that which you do not understand. Therefore for your sakes I will show **what conversion is.**

Others cherish secret hopes of mercy, though they continue as they are. For them I must show **the necessity of conversion.**

Others are likely to harden themselves with a vain conceit that they are converted already. To them I must show **the marks of the unconverted.**

Others, because they feel no harm, fear none, and so sleep as upon the top of a mast. To them I shall show **the misery of the unconverted.**

Others sit still, because they do not see the way of escape. To them I shall show **the means of conversion.**

And finally, for the quickening of all, I shall close with **the motives to conversion.**

1

Mistakes about conversion

The devil has made many counterfeits of conversion, and cheats one with this, and another with that. He has such craft and artifice in his mystery of deceits that, if it were possible, he would deceive the very elect. Now, that I may cure the ruinous mistake of some who think they are converted when they are not, as well as remove the troubles and fears of others who think they are not converted when they are, I shall show you the nature of conversion, both what it is not, and what it is. We will begin with the negative.

Conversion is not the taking upon us the profession of Christianity. Christianity is more than a name. If we will hear Paul, it does not lie in word, but in power (1 Cor iv 20). If to cease to be Jews and pagans, and to put on the Christian profession, had been true conversion – as this is all that some would have to be understood by it – who better Christians than they of Sardis and Laodicea? These were all Christians by profession, and had a name to live only; but because they had a name, they are condemned by Christ, and threatened to be rejected (Rev iii 14–16). Are there not many that name the name of the Lord Jesus, that do not depart from iniquity (2 Tim ii 19), and profess they know God, but in works deny Him? (Titus i 16). And will God receive these for true converts? What! converts from sin, when they still live in sin? It is a visible contradiction. Surely, if the lamp of profession would have served the turn, the foolish virgins had never been shut out (Mt xxv 12). We find not only professing Christians, but preachers of Christ, and wonder-workers, rejected, because they are evil-workers (Mt vii 22–23).

Conversion is not putting on the badge of Christ in baptism.
Ananias and Sapphira, and Simon Magus were baptized as well as
the rest. How many make a mistake here, deceiving and being
deceived; dreaming that effectual grace is necessarily tied to the
external administration of baptism, so that every baptized person
is regenerated, not only sacramentally, but really and properly.
Hence men fancy that because they were regenerated when
baptized, they need no farther work. But if this were so, then all
that have been baptized must necessarily be saved, because the
promise of pardon and salvation is made to conversion and regeneration (Acts iii 19; Mt xix 28). And indeed, were conversion and baptism the same, then men would do well to carry but a
certificate of their baptism when they died, and upon sight of this
there were no doubt of their admission into heaven.

In short, if there is nothing more to conversion, or regeneration, than to be baptized, this will fly directly in the face of that
Scripture, Mt vii 13–14, as well as multitudes of others. If this is
true, we shall no more say, '*Strait is the gate, and narrow is the
way*' for if all that are baptized are saved, the door is exceeding
wide, and we shall henceforth say, 'Wide is the gate, and broad
is the way that leadeth unto life.' If this is true, thousands may go
in abreast; and we will no more teach that the righteous are
scarcely saved, or that there is need of such a stir in taking the
kingdom of heaven by violence, and striving to enter in (1 Pet
iv 18; Mt xi 12; Lk xiii 24). Surely, if the way be so easy as
many suppose, that little more is necessary than to be baptized
and to cry out, 'Lord, have mercy', we need not put ourselves
to such seeking, and knocking, and wrestling, as the Word
requires in order to salvation. Again, if this is true, we shall no
more say, '*Few there be that find it*'; we will rather say, 'Few
there be that miss it.' We shall no more say, that of the many that
are called, only '*few are chosen*' (Mt xxii 14), and that even of
the professing Israel but a remnant shall be saved (Rom ix 27). If
this doctrine is true, we shall no more say with the disciples, '*Who

then shall be saved?' but rather, 'Who then shall not be saved?' Then, if a man be baptized, though he is a fornicator, or a railer or covetous, or a drunkard, yet he shall inherit the kingdom of God! (1 Cor v 11 and vi 9, 10).

But some will reply, 'Such as these, though they received regenerating grace in baptism, are since fallen away, and must be renewed again, or else they cannot be saved.'

I answer, 1. There is an infallible connection between regeneration and salvation, as we have already shown. 2. Then man must be again born again, which carries a great deal of absurdity in its face. We might as well expect men to be twice born in nature as twice born in grace! But, 3, and above all, this grants the thing I contend for, that whatever men do or pretend to receive in baptism, if they are found afterwards to be grossly ignorant, or profane, or formal, without the power of godliness, they *'must be born again'* (Jn iii 7) or else be shut out of the kingdom of God. So then they must have more to plead for themselves than their baptismal regeneration.

Well, in this you see all are agreed, that, be it more or less that is received in baptism, if men are evidently unsanctified, they must be renewed by a thorough and powerful change, or else they cannot escape the damnation of hell. *'Be not deceived; God is not mocked.'* Whether it be your baptism, or whatever else you pretend, I tell you from the living God, that if any of you be a prayerless person, or a scoffer, or a lover of evil company (Prov xiii 20), in a word, if you are not a holy, strict, and self-denying Christian, you cannot be saved (Heb xii 14; Mt xv 14).

Conversion does not lie in moral righteousness. This does not exceed the righteousness of the Scribes and Pharisees, and therefore cannot bring us to the kingdom of God (Mt v 20). Paul, while unconverted, touching the righteousness which is in the law was blameless (Phil iii 6). The Pharisee could say, 'I am no extortioner, adulterer, unjust', etc. (Lk xviii 11). You must have something more than all this to show, or else, however you may justify yourself, God will condemn you. I do not condemn morality, but I warn you not to rest in it. Piety includes morality, as Christianity does humanity, and as grace does reason; but we must not divide the tables.

Conversion does not consist in an external conformity to the rules of piety. It is manifest that men may have a form of godliness, without the power (2 Tim iii 5). Men may pray long (Mt xxiii 14), and fast often (Lk xviii 12), and hear gladly (Mk vi 20), and be very forward in the service of God, though costly and expensive (Is i 11), and yet be strangers to conversion. They must have more to plead for themselves than that they go to church, give alms, and make use of prayer, to prove themselves sound converts. There is no outward service but a hypocrite may do it, even to the giving of all his goods to feed the poor, and his body to be burned (1 Cor xiii 3).

Conversion is not the mere chaining up of corruption by education, human laws or the force of affliction. It is too common and easy to mistake education for grace; but if this were enough, who a better man than Jehoash? While Jehoiada, his uncle, lived, he was very forward in God's service, and calls upon him to repair the house of the Lord (2 Kgs xii 2, 7). But here was nothing more than good education all this while; for when his good tutor was taken away he appears to have been but a wolf chained up, and falls into idolatry.

In short, conversion does not consist in illumination or conviction or in a superficial change or partial reformation. An apostate may be an enlightened man (Heb vi 4), and a Felix tremble under conviction (Acts xxiv 25), and a Herod do many things (Mk vi 20). It is one thing to have sin alarmed only by convictions, and another to have it crucified by converting grace. Many, because they have been troubled in conscience for their sins, think well of their case, miserably mistaking conviction for conversion. With these, Cain might have passed for a convert, who ran up and down the world like a man distracted, under the rage of a guilty conscience, till he stifled it with building and business. Others think that because they have given up their riotous ways, and are broken off from evil company or some particular lust, and are reduced to sobriety and civility, they are now real converts. They forget that there is a vast difference between being sanctified and civilized. They forget that many seek to enter into the kingdom of heaven, and are not far from it, and arrive to the almost of Christianity, and yet fall short at last. While conscience holds the whip over them, many will pray, hear, read, and forbear their delightful sins; but no sooner is the lion asleep than they are at their sins again. Who more religious than the Jews when God's hand was upon them? Yet no sooner was the affliction over, than they forgot God. You may have forsaken a troublesome sin, and have escaped the gross pollutions of the world, and yet in all this not have changed your carnal nature.

You may take a crude mass of lead and mould it into the more comely proportion of a plant, and then into the shape of an animal, and then into the form and features of a man; but all the time it is still lead. So a man may pass through various transmutations, from ignorance to knowledge, from profanity to civility, then to a form of religion, and all this time he is still carnal and unregenerate, his nature remains unchanged.

Hear then, O sinners, hear as you would live. Why should you wilfully deceive yourselves, or build your hopes upon the sand? I know that he will find hard work that goes to pluck away your hopes. It cannot but be unpleasant to you, and truly it is not pleasing to me. I set about it as a surgeon when about to cut off a mortified limb from his beloved friend, which of necessity he must do, though with an aching heart. But understand me, beloved, I am only taking down the ruinous house, which otherwise will speedily fall of itself and bury you in the ruins, that I may build it fair, strong, and firm for ever. The hope of the wicked shall perish (Prov xi 7). And had you not better, O sinner, let the Word convince you now in time, and let go your false and self-deluding hopes, than have death open your eyes too late, and find yourself in hell before you are aware? I should be a false and faithless shepherd if I should not tell you, that you who have built your hopes upon no better grounds than these before mentioned, are yet in your sins. Let conscience speak. What have you to plead for yourselves? Is it that you wear Christ's livery; that you bear His name; that you are a member of the visible church; that you have knowledge in the points of religion, are civilized, perform religious duties, are just in your dealings, have been troubled in conscience for your sins? I tell you from the Lord, these pleas will never be accepted at God's bar. All this, though good in itself, will not prove you converted, and so will not suffice to your salvation. O look to it, and resolve to turn speedily and entirely. Study your own hearts; do not rest till God has made thorough work with you; for you must be other men, or else you are lost men.

But if these persons come short of conversion, what shall I say of the profane person? It may be he will scarcely cast his eyes on, or lend his ear to this discourse; but if there be any such reading, or within hearing, he must know from the Lord that made him, that he is far from the kingdom of God. May a man keep company with the wise virgins, and yet be shut out; and shall not a companion of fools much more be destroyed? May a man be true in his dealings, and yet not be justified before God? What then will become of you, O wretched man, whose conscience tells you that you are false in your trade and false to your word? If men may be enlightened and brought to the external performance of holy duties, and yet go down to perdition for resting in them and sitting down on this side of conversion; what will become of you, O miserable families that live without God in the world? What will become of you, O wretched sinners, with whom God is scarcely in all your thoughts; that are so ignorant that you cannot pray, or so careless that you will not? O repent and be converted, break off your sins by righteousness. Away to Christ for pardoning and renewing grace. Give up yourselves to Him, to walk with Him in holiness, or you shall never see God. O that you would heed the warnings of God! In His name I once more admonish you. Turn ye at my reproof. Forsake the foolish, and live. Be sober, righteous, and godly. Wash your hands, ye sinners; purify your hearts, ye double-minded. Cease to do evil, learn to do well (Prov i 23 and ix 6; Tit ii 12; Jas iv 8; Is i 16–17). But if you will go on, you must die.

2

The nature of conversion

I dare not leave you with your eyes half open, like him that saw
'men as trees walking'. The Word is profitable for doctrine as
well as reproof. And therefore, having thus far conducted you by
the shelves and rocks of so many dangerous mistakes, I would
guide you at length into the haven of truth.

Conversion then, in short, lies in the thorough change both of
the heart and life. I shall briefly describe it in its nature and
causes.

1: The Author of conversion is the Spirit of God, and therefore
it is called *'the sanctification of the Spirit'* (2 Thess ii 13) and
'the renewing of the Holy Ghost' (Tit iii 5). This does not exclude
the other persons in the Trinity, for the apostle teaches us to
bless the Father of our Lord Jesus Christ, who *'hath begotten
us again unto a lively hope'* (1 Pet i 3). And Christ is said to
'give repentance unto Israel' (Acts v 31); and is called the *'everlasting Father'* (Is ix 6) and we His seed, and *'the children which
God hath given Him'* (Heb ii 13). Yet this work is principally
ascribed to the Holy Ghost, and so we are said to be *'born of
the Spirit'* (Jn iii 5–6).

So then, conversion is a work above man's power. We are
*'born, not of blood, nor of the will of the flesh, nor of the will of
man, but of God'* (Jn i 13). Never think you can convert yourself.
If ever you would be savingly converted, you must despair of
doing it in your own strength. It is a resurrection from the dead
(Eph ii 1) a new creation (Gal vi 15; Eph ii 10), a work of

absolute omnipotence (Eph i 19). Are not these out of the reach of human power? If you have no more than you had by your first birth, a good nature, a meek and chaste temper etc., you are a stranger to true conversion. This is a supernatural work.

2: The efficient cause of conversion is both internal and external.

[1] **The internal cause** is free grace alone. '*Not by works of righteousness which we have done, but of his mercy he saved us*', and '*by the renewing of the Holy Ghost*' (Tit iii 5). '*Of his own will begat he us*' (Jas i 18). We are chosen and called unto sanctification, not for it (Eph i 4).

God finds nothing in man to turn His heart, but enough to turn His stomach; He finds enough to provoke His loathing, but nothing to excite His love. Look back upon yourself, O Christian! Reflect upon your swinish nature, your filthy swill, your once beloved mire (2 Pet 2). Behold your slime and corruption. Do not your own clothes abhor you? (Job ix 31). How then should holiness and purity love you? Be astonished, O heavens, at this; be moved, O earth. Who but must needs cry, Grace! Grace! (Zech iv 7). Hear and blush, you children of the Most High. O unthankful men, that free grace is no more in your mouths, in your thoughts; no more adored, admired and commended by such as you! One would think you should be doing nothing but praising and admiring God wherever you are. How can you forget such grace, or pass it over with a slight and formal mention? What but free grace could move God to love you, unless enmity could do it, unless deformity could do it? How affectionately Peter lifts up his hands, '*Blessed be the God and Father of our Lord Jesus, who of his abundant mercy hath begotten us again.*' How feelingly does Paul magnify the free mercy of God in it, '*God who is rich in mercy, for his great love wherewith he loved us, hath quickened us together with Christ. By grace are ye saved*' (Eph ii 4–5)!

[2] **The external cause** is the merit and intercession of the blessed Jesus. He has obtained gifts for the rebellious (Ps lxviii 18), and through Him it is that God worketh in us that which is

well-pleasing in His sight (Heb xiii 21). Through Him are all spiritual blessings bestowed upon us in heavenly places (Eph i 3). He intercedes for the elect that believe not (Jn xvii 20). Every convert is the fruit of His travail. Never was an infant born into the world with that difficulty which Christ endured for us. All the pains that He suffered on the cross were our birth-pains. He is made sanctification to us (1 Cor i 30). He sanctified Himself, that is, set apart Himself as a sacrifice, that we might be sanctified (Jn xvii 19). We are sanctified through the offering of His body once for all (Heb x 10).

It is nothing, then, but the merit and intercession of Christ, that prevails with God to bestow on us converting grace. If you are a new creature, you know to whom you owe it; to Christ's pangs and prayers. The foal does not more naturally run after the dam, nor the suckling to the breast, than a believer to Jesus Christ. And where else should you go? If any in the world can show for your heart what Christ can let them do it. Does Satan claim you? Does the world court you? Does sin sue for your heart? Why, were these crucified for you? O Christian, love and serve your Lord while you have a being.

3: The instrument of conversion is personal and real.

[1] **The personal instrument** is the ministry. '*In Christ Jesus I have begotten you through the gospel*' (1 Cor iv 15). Christ's ministers are they that are sent to open men's eyes, and to turn them to God (Acts xxvi 18). O unthankful world! Little do you know what you are doing when you are persecuting the messengers of the Lord. These are they whose business it is, under Christ, to save you. Whom have you reproached and blasphemed? (Is xxxvii 23). These are the servants of the most high God that show unto you the way of salvation (Acts xvi 17), and do you requite them thus, O foolish and unwise? (Deut xxxii 6). O sons of ingratitude, against whom do you sport yourselves? These are the instruments that God uses to convert and save sinners: and do you revile your physicians, and throw your pilots

overboard? '*Father, forgive them; for they know not what they do.*'

[2] **The real instrument** is the Word. We are begotten by the word of truth. It is this that enlightens the eye, that converts the soul (Ps xix 7, 8), that makes us wise to salvation (2 Tim iii 15). This is the incorruptible seed by which we are born again (1 Pet i 23). If we are washed, it is by the Word (Eph v 26). If we are sanctified, it is through the truth (Jn xvii 17). This generates faith, and regenerates us (Rom x 17; Jas i 18).

O ye saints, how you should love the Word, for by this you have been converted! You that have felt its renewing power, make much of it while you live; be ever thankful for it. Tie it about your neck, write it upon your hand, lay it in your bosom. When you go let it lead you, when you sleep let it keep you, when you wake let it talk with you (Prov vi 21–22). Say with the Psalmist, '*I will never forget thy precepts, for by them thou hast quickened me*' (Ps cxix 93). You that are unconverted, read the Word with diligence; flock to where it is powerfully preached. Pray for the coming of the Spirit in the Word. Come from your knees to the sermon, and come from the sermon to your knees. The sermon does not prosper because it is not watered by prayers and tears, nor covered by meditation.

4: The final cause or end of conversion is man's salvation, and God's glory. We are chosen through sanctification to salvation (2 Thess ii 13), called that we might be glorified (Rom viii 30), but especially that God might be glorified (Is lx 21), that we should show forth His praises (1 Pet ii 9), and be fruitful in good works (Col i 10).

O Christian, do not forget the end of your calling. Let your light shine, let your lamp burn, let your fruits be good and many and in season (Ps i 3). Let all your designs fall in with God's, that He may be magnified in you (Phil i 20).

5: The subject of conversion is the elect sinner, and that in all his parts and powers, members and mind. Whom God predestinates, them only He calls (Rom viii 30). None are drawn to Christ by their calling, nor come to Him by believing, but His sheep, those whom the Father has given Him (Jn vi 37, 44). Effectual calling runs parallel with eternal election (2 Pet i 10).

You begin at the wrong end if you first dispute about your election. Prove your conversion, and then never doubt your election. If you cannot yet prove it, set upon a present and thorough turning. Whatever God's purposes be, which are secret, I am sure His promises are plain. How desperately do rebels argue! 'If I am elected I shall be saved, do what I will. If not, I shall be damned, do what I can.' Perverse sinner, will you begin where you should end? Is not the word before you? What saith it? *'Repent and be converted, that your sins may be blotted out.' 'If you mortify the deeds of the body you shall live.' 'Believe and be saved'* (Acts iii 19: Rom viii 13; Acts xvi 31). What can be plainer? Do not stand still disputing about your election, but set to repenting and believing. Cry to God for converting grace. Revealed things belong to you; in these busy yourself. It is just, as one well said, that they who will not feed on the plain food of the Word should be choked with the bones. Whatever God's purposes may be, I am sure His promises are true. Whatever the decrees of heaven may be, I am sure that if I repent and believe I shall be saved; and that if I do not repent, I shall be damned. Is not this plain ground for you; and will you yet run upon the rocks?

More particularly, this change of conversion extends to the whole man. A carnal person may have some shreds of good morality, but he is never good throughout the whole cloth. Conversion is not a repairing of the old building; but it takes all down, and erects a new structure. It is not the sewing on a patch of holiness; but with the true convert, holiness is woven into all his powers, principles and practice. The sincere Christian is quite a new fabric, from the foundation to the top-stone. He is a new man, a new creature; all things are become new (2 Cor v 17). Conversion is a deep work, a heart work. It makes a new man in a new world. It extends to the whole man, to the mind, to the members, to the motions of the whole life.

[1] **The mind.**

Conversion turns the balance of the judgment, so that God and His glory outweigh all carnal and worldly interests. It opens the eye of the mind, and makes the scales of its native ignorance fall off, and turns men from darkness to light. The man that before saw no danger in his condition, now concludes himself lost and for ever undone (Acts ii 37) except renewed by the power of grace. He that formerly thought there was little hurt in sin, now comes to see it to be the chief of evils. He sees the unreasonableness, the unrighteousness, the deformity and the filthiness of sin; so that he is affrighted with it, loathes it, dreads it, flees from it, and even abhors himself for it (Rom vii 15; Job xlii 6; Ezek xxxvi 31). He that could see little sin in himself, and could find no matter for confession, now sees the rottenness of his heart, the desperate and deep pollution of his whole nature. He cries, 'Unclean! Unclean! Lord, purge me with hyssop, wash me thoroughly, create in me a clean heart.' He sees himself altogether filthy, corrupt both root and branch (Ps xiv 3; Mt vii 17–18). He writes 'unclean' upon all his parts, and powers, and performances (Is lxiv 6; Rom vii 18). He discovers the filthy corners that he was never aware of, and sees the blasphemy, and theft, and murder, and adultery, that is in his heart, of which before he was ignorant. Hitherto he saw no form nor comeliness in Christ, no beauty that he should desire Him; but now he finds the Hidden Treasure, and will sell all to buy this field. Christ is the Pearl he seeks.

Now, according to this new light, the man is of another mind, another judgment, than he was before. Now God is all with him, he has none in heaven nor in earth like Him; he truly prefers Him before all the world. His favour is his life, the light of His countenance is more than corn and wine and oil (the good that he formerly enquired after, and set his heart upon. Ps iv 6–7). A hypocrite may come to yield a general assent that God is the chief good; indeed, the wiser heathens, some few of them, have at least stumbled upon this. But no hypocrite comes so far as to look upon God as the most desirable and suitable good to him, and thereupon to acquiesce in Him. This is the convert's voice: *'The Lord is my portion, saith my soul. Whom have I in heaven but thee? and there is none upon earth that I desire beside thee. God is the strength of my heart and my portion for ever'* (Lam iii 24; Ps lxxiii 25–26).

Conversion turns the bias of the will both as to means and end. The intentions of the will are altered. Now the man has new ends and designs. He now intends God above all, and desires and designs nothing in all the world, so much as that Christ may be magnified in him. He counts himself more happy in this than in all that the earth could yield, that he may be serviceable to Christ, and bring Him glory. This is the mark he aims at, that the name of Jesus may be great in the world.

Reader, do you read this without asking yourself whether it be thus with you? Pause a while, and examine yourself.

The choice is also changed. He pitches upon God as his blessedness, and upon Christ and holiness as means to bring him to God. He chooses Jesus for his Lord. He is not merely forced to Christ by the storm, nor does he take Christ for bare necessity, but he comes freely. His choice is not made in a fright, as with the terrified conscience, or the dying sinner that will seemingly do anything for Christ, but only takes Christ rather than hell. He deliberately resolves that Christ is his best choice, and would rather have Him than all the good of this world, might he enjoy it while he would (Phil i 23). Again, he takes holiness for his path; he does not out of mere necessity submit to it, but he likes it and loves it. *'I have chosen the way of thy precepts'* (Ps cxix 173). He takes God's testimonies not as his bondage, but his heritage; yea, heritage for ever. He counts them not his burden, but his bliss; not his cords, but his cordials (1 Jn v 3; Ps cxix 14, 16, 47). He does not only bear, but takes up Christ's yoke. He takes not holiness as the stomach does the loathed medicine, which a man will take rather than die, but as the hungry man does his beloved food. No time passes so sweetly with him, when he is himself, as that which he spends in the exercises of holiness. These are both his aliment and element, the desire of his eyes and the joy of his heart.

Put it to your conscience whether you are the man. O happy man, if this be your case! But see that you are thorough and impartial in the search.

Conversion turns the bent of the affections. These all run in a new channel. The Jordan is now driven back, and the water runs upwards against its natural course. Christ is his hope. This is his prize. Here his eye is: here his heart. He is content to cast all overboard, as the merchant in the storm about to perish, so he may but keep this jewel.

The first of his desires is not after gold, but grace. He hungers for it, he seeks it as silver, he digs for it as for hid treasure. He had rather be gracious than great. He had rather be the holiest man on earth than the most learned, the most famous, the most prosperous. While carnal, he said, 'O if I were but in great esteem, rolling in wealth, and swimming in pleasure; if my debts were paid, and I and mine provided for, then I would be a happy man.' But now the tune is changed. 'Oh!' says the convert, 'if I had but my corruptions subdued, if I had such a measure of grace, and fellowship with God, though I were poor and despised I should not care, I should account myself a blessed man.' Reader, is this the language of your soul?

His joys are changed. He rejoices in the way of God's testimonies as much as in all riches. He delights in the law of the Lord, in which he once had little savour. He has no such joy as in the thoughts of Christ, the enjoyment of His company, the prosperity of His people.

His cares are quite altered. He was once set for the world, and any scrap of spare-time was enough for his soul. Now his cry is, *'What must I do to be saved?'* (Acts xvi 30). His great concern is how to secure his soul. O how he would bless you, if you could but put him out of doubt concerning this!

[33]

His fears are not so much of suffering as of sinning. Once he was afraid of nothing so much as the loss of his estate or reputation; nothing sounded so terrible to him as pain, or poverty, or disgrace. Now these are little to him, in comparison with God's dishonour or displeasure. How warily does he walk, lest he should tread upon a snare! He looks in front, and behind: he has his eye upon his heart, and is often casting it over his shoulder, lest he should be overtaken with sin. It kills his heart to think of losing God's favour; this he dreads as his only undoing. No thought pains him so much as to think of parting with Christ.

His love runs in a new course. 'My Love was crucified', says Ignatius, that is, my Christ. '*This is my beloved*', says the spouse (Cant v 16). How often does Augustine pour his love upon Christ! He can find no words sweet enough. 'Let me see Thee, O Light of mine eyes. Come, O Thou Joy of my spirit; Let me behold Thee, O Gladness of my heart. Let me love Thee, O Life of my soul. Appear unto me, O my great delight, my sweet comfort, O my God, my life, and the whole glory of my soul. Let me find Thee, O Desire of my heart; let me hold Thee, O Love of my soul. Let me embrace Thee, O Heavenly Bridegroom. Let me possess Thee.'

His sorrows have now a new vent (2 Cor vii 9–10). The view of his sins, the sight of Christ crucified, that could scarcely stir him before, now how much do they affect his heart!

His hatred boils, his anger burns against sin. He has no patience with himself; he calls himself fool, and beast, and thinks any name too good for himself, when his indignation is stirred up against sin (Ps lxxiii 22; Prov xxx 2). He could once wallow in it with much pleasure; now he loathes the thought of returning to it as much as of licking up the filthiest vomit.

Commune then with your own heart, and attend to the general current of your affections, whether they be towards God in Christ above all other concerns. Indeed, sudden and strong motions of the affections are often found in hypocrites, especially where the natural temperament is warm. And contrariwise, the sanctified themselves are often without conscious stirring of the affections, where the temperament is more slow, dry, and dull. The great inquiry is, whether the judgment and will are steadily determined for God above all other good, real or apparent. If so, and if the affections do sincerely follow their choice and conduct, though it be not so strongly and feelingly as is to be desired, there is no doubt but the change is saving.

[2] **The members.**

These that before were the instruments of sin, are now become the holy utensils of Christ's living temple. He that before dishonoured his body, now possesses his vessel in sanctification and honour, in temperance, chastity, and sobriety, and dedicates it to the Lord.

The eye, that was once a wandering eye, a wanton eye, a haughty, a covetous eye, is now employed, as Mary's, in weeping over its sins, in beholding God in His works, in reading His Word, or in looking for objects of mercy and opportunities for His service.

The ear, that was once open to Satan's call, and that did relish nothing so much as filthy, or at least frothy talk, and the laughter of fools, is now bored to the door of Christ's house, and open to His disciples. It says, '*Speak, Lord, for thy servant heareth.*' It waits for His words as the rain, and relishes them more than the appointed food (Job xxiii 12), more than the honey and the honeycomb (Ps xix 10).

The head, that was full of worldly designs, is now filled with other matters, and set on the study of God's will, and the man employs his head, not so much about his gain as about his duty. The thoughts and cares that fill his head are, principally, how he may please God and flee sin.

His heart, that was a sty of filthy lusts, is now become an altar of incense, where the fire of divine love is ever kept burning, and from which the daily sacrifice of prayer and praise, and the sweet incense of holy desires, ejaculations and prayers, are continually ascending.

The mouth is become a well of life; his tongue as choice silver, and his lips feed many. Now the salt of grace has seasoned his speech, has eaten out the corruption (Col iv 6), and cleansed the man from his filthy conversation, flattery, boasting, railing, lying, swearing, backbiting, that once came like flashes proceeding from the hell that was in the heart (Jas iii 6). The throat, that once was an open sepulchre, now sends forth the sweet breath of prayer and holy discourse, and the man speaks in another tongue, in the language of Canaan, and is never so well as when talking of God and Christ, and the matters of another world. His mouth brings forth wisdom; his tongue is become the silver trumpet of his Maker's praise, his glory and the best member that he has.

Now here you will find the hypocrite sadly deficient. He speaks, it may be, like an angel, but he has a covetous eye, or the gain of unrighteousness is in his hand. His hand is white, but his heart is full of rottenness (Mt xxiii 27), full of unmortified cares, a very oven of lust, a shop of pride, the seat of malice. It may be, with Nebuchadnezzar's image, he has a golden head – a great deal of knowledge; but he has feet of clay – his affections are worldly, he minds earthly things, and his way and walk are sensual and carnal. The work is not thorough with him.

[3] **The life and practice.**

The new man takes a new course (Eph ii 2–3). His conversation is in heaven (Phil iii 20). No sooner does Christ call by effectual grace but he straightway becomes a follower of Him. When God has given the new heart, and written His law in his mind, he henceforth walks in His statutes and keeps His judgments.

Though sin may dwell in him – truly a wearisome and unwelcome guest – yet it has no more dominion over him. He has his fruit unto holiness, and though he makes many a blot, yet the law and life of Jesus is what he looks at as his pattern, and he has an unfeigned respect to all God's commandments. He makes conscience even of little sins and little duties. His very infirmities which he cannot help, though he would, are his soul's burden, and are like dust in a man's eye, which though but little, is not a little troublesome. (O man, do you read this, and never stop to examine yourself?) The sincere convert is not one man at church and another at home. He is not a saint on his knees and a cheat in his shop. He will not tithe mint and cummin, and neglect mercy and judgment, and the weightier matters of the law. He does not pretend piety and neglect morality. But he turns from all his sins and keeps all God's statutes, though not perfectly, except in desire and endeavour, yet sincerely, not allowing himself in the breach of any. Now he delights in the Word, and sets himself to prayer, and opens his hand and draws out his soul to the hungry. He breaks off his sins by righteousness, and his iniquities by showing mercy to the poor (Dan iv 27). He has a good conscience willing in all things to live honestly (Heb xiii 18), and to keep without offence towards God and men.

Here again you find the unsoundness of many that take themselves for good Christians. They are partial in the law (Mal ii 9), and take up the cheap and easy duties of religion, but they do not go through with the work. They are as a cake half-baked and half-raw. It may be you find them exact in their words, punctual in their dealings, but then they do not exercise themselves unto godliness; and as for examining themselves and governing their hearts, to this they are strangers. You may see them duly at church; but follow them to their families, and there you shall see little but the world minded; or if they have family duties, follow them to their closets, and there you shall find their souls are little looked after. It may be that they seem religious, but they do not bridle their tongues, and so all their religion is vain (Jas i 26). It may be they come to closet and family prayer; but follow them to their shops, and there you find them in the habit of lying, or some fashionable way of deceit. Thus the hypocrite is not thorough in his obedience.

6. The objects from which we turn in conversion are, sin, Satan, the world, and our own righteousness.

[1] We turn from sin. When a man is converted, he is for ever at

enmity with sin; yes, with all sin, but most of all with his own sins, and especially with his bosom sin. Sin is now the object of his indignation. His sin swells his sorrows. It is sin that pierces him and wounds him; he feels it like a thorn in his side, like a prick in his eyes. He groans and struggles under it, and not formally, but feelingly cries out, '*O wretched man!*' He is not impatient of any burden so much as of his sin. If God should give him his choice, he would choose any affliction so he might be rid of sin; he feels it like the cutting gravel in his shoes, pricking and paining him as he goes.

Before conversion he had light thoughts of sin. He cherished it in his bosom, as Uriah his lamb; he nourished it up, and it grew up together with him; it did eat, as it were, of his own meat and drank of his own cup, and lay in his bosom, and was to him as a daughter. But when God opens his eyes by conversion, he throws it away with abhorrence, as a man would a loathsome toad, which in the dark he had hugged fast in his bosom, and thought it had been some pretty and harmless bird. When a man is savingly changed, he is deeply convinced not only of the danger but the defilement of sin; and O, how earnest is he with God to be purified! He loathes himself for his sins. He runs to Christ, and casts himself into the fountain set open for him and for unclean-ness. If he fall, what a stir is there to get all clean again! He has no rest till he flees to the Word, and washes and rubs and rinses in the infinite fountain, labouring to cleanse himself from all filthi-ness both of flesh and spirit.

The sound convert is heartily engaged against sin. He struggles with it, he wars against it; he is too often foiled, but he will never yield the cause, nor lay down the weapons, while he has breath in his body. He will make no peace; he will give no quarter. He can forgive his other enemies, he can pity them and pray for them; but here he is implacable, here he is set upon their exter-mination. He hunts as it were for the precious life; his eye shall not pity, his hand shall not spare, though it be a right hand or a right eye. Be it a gainful sin, most delightful to his nature or the support of his esteem with worldly friends, yet he will rather throw his gain down the gutter, see his credit fail, or the flower of his pleasure wither in his hand, than he will allow himself in any known way of sin. He will grant no indulgence, he will give no toleration. He draws upon sin wherever he meets it, and frowns upon it with this unwelcome salute, 'Have I found thee, O mine enemy?'

Reader, has conscience been at work while you have been looking over these lines? Have you pondered these things in your heart? Have you searched the book within, to see if these things be so? If not, read it again, and make your conscience speak, whether or not it is thus with you.

Have you crucified your flesh with its affections and lusts; and not only confessed, but forsaken your sins, all sin in your fervent desires, and the ordinary practice of every deliberate and wilful sin in your life? If not, you are yet unconverted. Does not conscience fly in your face as you read, and tell you that you live in a way of lying for your advantage? that you use deceit in your calling? that there is some way of secret wantonness that you live in? Why then, do not deceive yourself. *'Thou art in the gall of bitterness and the bond of iniquity.'*

Does your unbridled tongue, your indulgence of appetite, your wicked company, your neglect of prayer, of reading and hearing the Word, now witness against you, and say, 'We are your works, and we will follow you'? Or, if I have not hit you right, does not the monitor within tell you, there is such and such a way that you know to be evil, that yet for some carnal respect you tolerate in yourself? If this be the case, you are to this day unregenerate, and must be changed or condemned.

[2] **We turn from Satan.** Conversion binds the strong man, spoils his armour, casts out his goods, turns men from the power of Satan unto God. Before, the devil could no sooner hold up his finger to the sinner to call him to his wicked company, sinful games, and filthy delights, but immediately he followed, *'as an ox goeth to the slaughter, or as a fool to the correction of the stocks;*

as the bird that hasteth to the snare and knoweth not that it is for his life' (Prov vii 22–23). No sooner could Satan bid him lie, but immediately he had it on his tongue. No sooner could Satan offer a wanton object, but he was stung with lust. If the devil says, 'Away with these family duties', be sure they shall be rarely performed in his house. If the devil says, 'Away with this strictness, this preciseness' he will keep far enough from it. If he tells him, 'There is no need of these secret-duties', he will go from day to day and scarcely perform them. But after he is converted he serves another Master, and takes quite another course; he goes and comes at Christ's bidding. Satan may sometimes catch his foot in a trap, but he will no longer be a willing captive. He watches against the snares and baits of Satan, and studies to be acquainted with his devices. He is very suspicious of his plots, and is very jealous in what comes across him, lest Satan should have some design upon him. He wrestles against principalities and powers; he entertains the messenger of Satan as men do the messenger of death. He keeps his eye upon his enemy, and watches in his duties, lest Satan should get an advantage.

[3] **We turn from the world.** Before a man has true faith, he is overcome by the world. He either bows down to mammon, or idolizes his reputation, or is a lover of pleasure more than a lover of God. Here is the root of man's misery by the fall. He is turned aside to the creature, and gives that esteem, confidence and affection to the creature that is due to God alone.

O miserable man, what a deformed monster has sin made you! God made you *'little lower than the angels'*; sin has made you little better than the devils, a monster that has his head and his heart where his feet should be, and his feet kicking against heaven, and everything out of place. The world that was formed to serve you, is come up to rule you – the deceitful harlot has bewitched you with her enchantments, and made you bow down and serve her.

But converting grace sets all in order again, and puts God on the throne, and the world at his footstool; Christ in the heart, and the world under the feet. '*I am crucified to the world, and the world to me*' (Gal vi 14). Before this change, all the cry was '*Who will show us any* (worldly) *good?*' but now he prays, '*Lord, lift thou up the light of thy countenance upon me*', and take the corn and wine whosoever will (Ps iv 6–7). Before, his heart's delight and content were in the world; then the song was, '*Soul, take thine ease, eat, drink, and be merry; thou hast much goods laid up for many years.*' But now all this is withered, and there is no comeliness, that we should desire it; and he tunes up with the sweet psalmist of Israel, '*The Lord is the portion of my inheritance; the lines are fallen to me in a fair place, and I have a goodly heritage.*' Nothing else can make him content. He has written vanity and vexation upon all his worldly enjoyments, and loss and dung upon all human excellencies. He has life and immortality now in pursuit. He pants for grace and glory, and has a crown incorruptible in view. His heart is set in him to seek the Lord. He first seeks the kingdom of God and His righteousness, and religion is no longer a casual matter with him, but his main care. Before, the world had the sway with him. He would do more for gain than godliness – more to please his friend or his flesh, than the God that made him; and God must stand by till the world was first served. But now all must stand by; he hates father and mother, and life, and all, in comparison of Christ.

Well then, pause a little, and look within. Does not this concern you? You pretend to be for Christ, but does not the world sway you? Do you not take more real delight and content in the world than in Him? Do you not find yourself more at ease when the world is in your mind and you are surrounded with carnal delights, than when retired to prayer and meditation in your room, or attending upon God's Word and worship? There is no surer evidence of an unconverted state than to have the things of the world uppermost in our aim, love and estimation.

With the sound convert, Christ has the supremacy. How dear is His name to him! How precious is His favour! The name of Jesus is engraved on his heart. Honour is but air, and laughter is but madness, and mammon is fallen like Dagon before the ark, with hands and head broken off on the threshold, when once Christ is savingly revealed. Here is the pearl of great price to the true convert; here is his treasure; here is his hope. This is his glory, '*My beloved is mine, and I am his.*' O, it is sweeter to him to be able to say, 'Christ is mine', than if he could say, 'The kingdom is mine; the Indies are mine.'

[4] **We turn from our own righteousness.** Before conversion, man seeks to cover himself with his own fig-leaves, and to make himself whole with his own duties. He is apt to trust in himself, and set up his own righteousness, and to reckon his counters for gold, and not to submit to the righteousness of God. But conversion changes his mind; now he counts his own righteousness as filthy rags. He casts it off, as a man would the verminous tatters of a nasty beggar. Now he is brought to poverty of spirit, complains of and condemns himself, and all his inventory is, '*poor, and miserable, and wretched, and blind, and naked*'. He sees a world of iniquity in his holy things, and calls his once-idolized righteousness but filth and loss; and would not for a thousand worlds be found in it. Now he begins to set a high price upon Christ's righteousness. He sees the need of Christ in every duty, to justify his person and sanctify his performances; he cannot live without Him; he cannot pray without Him. Christ must go with him, or else he cannot come into the presence of God; he leans upon Christ, and so bows himself in the house of his God. He sets himself down for a lost undone man without Him; his life is hid in Christ, as the root of a tree spreads in the earth for stability and nourishment. Before, the news of Christ was a stale and tasteless thing; but now, how sweet is Christ! Augustine could not relish his once-admired Cicero, because he could not find in his writings the name of Christ. How emphatically he cries, 'O most sweet, most loving, most kind, most dear, most precious, most desired, most lovely, most fair!' (Meditat c 37) all in a breath, when he speaks of and to Christ. In a word, the voice of the convert is, with the martyr, 'None but Christ.'

7: The object to which we turn in conversion is, God the Father, Son, and Holy Ghost, whom the true convert takes as his all-sufficient and eternal blessedness. A man is never truly sanctified till his heart be truly set upon God above all things, as his portion and chief good. These are the natural breathings of a believer's heart: '*Thou art my portion.*' '*My soul shall make her boast in the Lord.*' '*My expectation is from him; he only is my rock and salvation and my glory; the rock of my strength, and my refuge, is in God*' (Ps cxix 57; Ps xxxiv 2; Ps lxii).

Would you be certain whether you are converted or not? Now let your soul and all that is within you attend.

Have you taken God for your happiness? Where does the desire of your heart lie? What is the source of your greatest satisfaction? Come, then, and with Abraham lift up your eyes eastward, and westward, and northward, and southward, and look around you; what is it that you would have in heaven or on earth to make you happy? If God should give you your choice, as He did to Solomon, or should say to you, as Ahasuerus to Esther, '*What is thy petition, and what is thy request, and it shall be granted thee?*' what would you ask? Go into the gardens of pleasure, and gather all the fragrant flowers there, would these satisfy you? Go to the treasures of mammon; suppose you may carry away as much as you desire. Go to the towers, to the trophies of honour. What do you think of being a man of renown, and having a name like the name of the great men of the earth? Would any of these, would all of these satisfy you, and make you to count yourself happy? If so, then certainly you are carnal and unconverted. If not, go farther; wade into the divine excellencies, the store of His mercies, the hiding of His power, the depths unfathomable of His all-sufficiency. Does this suit you best and please you most? Do you say, 'It is good to be here. Here will I pitch, here will I live and die'? Will you let all the world go rather than this? Then it is well between God and you: happy art thou, O man – happy art thou that ever thou wast born. If God can make you happy, you must be happy; for you have taken the Lord to be your God. Do you say to Christ as He to us, 'Thy Father shall be my Father, and thy God my God'? Here is the turning point. An unsound convert never takes up his rest in God; but converting grace does the work, and so cures the fatal misery of the fall, by turning the heart from its idol to the living God. Now the soul says, '*Lord, whither shall I go? Thou hast the words of eternal life.*' Here he centres, here he settles. It is the entrance of heaven to him; he sees his interest in God. When he discovers this, he says, '*Return unto thy rest, O my soul, for the Lord hath dealt bountifully with thee*' (Ps cxvi 7). And he is even ready to breathe out Simeon's song, '*Lord, now letteth thou thy servant depart in peace*'; and says with Jacob, when his old heart revived at the welcome tidings, '*It is enough*' (Gen xlv 28). When he sees he has a God in covenant to go to, this is all his salvation, and all his desire (2 Sam xxiii 5).

Is this the case with you? Have you experienced this? If so, then 'blessed art thou of the Lord'. God has been at work with you; He has laid hold of your heart by the power of converting grace, or else you could never have done this.

More particularly, in conversion.

[1] **We turn to Christ,** the only Mediator between God and man (1 Tim ii 5). His work is to bring us to God (1 Pet iii 18). He is the way to the Father (Jn xiv 6), the only plank on which we may escape, the only door by which we may enter (Jn x 9). Conversion brings the soul to Christ to accept Him as the only means of life, as the only way, the only name given under heaven. He does not look for salvation in any other but Him; he throws himself on Christ alone.

'Here', says the convinced sinner, 'I will venture; and if I perish, I perish; if I die, I will die here. But, Lord do not let me perish under the eye of Thy mercy. Entreat me not to leave Thee, or to return from following after Thee. Here I will throw myself; if Thou slay me, I will not go from Thy door.'

Thus the poor soul ventures on Christ and resolvedly adheres to Him. Before conversion, the man made light of Christ, minded his farm, friends, merchandise, more than Christ; now, Christ is to him as his necessary food, his daily bread, the life of his heart, the staff of his life. His great desire is, that Christ may be magnified in him. His heart once said, as they to the spouse, '*What is thy beloved more than another?*' (Cant v 9). He found more sweetness in his merry company, wicked games, earthly delights, than in Christ. He took religion for a fancy, and the talk of great enjoyments for an idle dream; but now to him to live is Christ. He sets light by all that he accounted precious, for the excellency of the knowledge of Christ.

All of Christ is accepted by the sincere convert. He loves not only the wages but the work of Christ, not only the benefits but the burden of Christ. He is willing not only to tread out the corn, but to draw under the yoke. He takes up the commands of Christ, yes, the cross of Christ.

The unsound convert takes Christ by halves. He is all for the salvation of Christ, but he is not for sanctification. He is for the privileges, but does not appropriate the person of Christ. He divides the offices and benefits of Christ. This is an error in the foundation. Whoever loves life, let him beware here. It is an undoing mistake, of which you have been often warned, and yet none is more common. Jesus is a sweet Name, but men do not love the Lord Jesus in sincerity. They will not have Him as God offers, '*to be a Prince and a Saviour*' (Acts v 31). They divide what God has joined, the King and the Priest. They will not accept the salvation of Christ as He intends it; they divide it here. Every man's vote is for salvation from suffering, but they do not desire to be saved from sinning. They would have their lives saved, but still would have their lusts. Indeed, many divide here again; they would be content to have some of their sins destroyed, but they cannot leave the lap of Delilah, or divorce the beloved Herodias. They cannot be cruel to the right eye or right hand. O be infinitely careful here; your soul depends upon it. The sound convert takes a whole Christ, and takes Him for all intents and purposes, without exceptions, without limitations, without reserve. He is willing to have Christ upon any terms; he is willing to have the dominion of Christ as well as deliverance by Christ. He says with Paul, '*Lord, what wilt thou have me to do?*' Anything, Lord. He sends the blank for Christ to set down His own conditions.

[2] **We turn to the laws, ordinances, and ways of Christ.** The heart that once was set against these, and could not endure the strictness of these bonds, the severity of these ways, now falls in love with them, and chooses them as its rule and guide for ever.

Four things, I observe, God works in every sound convert, with reference to the laws and ways of Christ, by which you may come to know your state, if you will be faithful to your own souls. Therefore, keep your eyes upon your hearts as you go along.

(i) **The judgment** is brought to approve of them and to subscribe to them as most righteous and most reasonable. The mind is brought to like the ways of God, and the corrupt prejudices that were once against them as unreasonable and intolerable, are now removed. The understanding assents to them all as holy, just, and good (Rom vii 12). How is David taken up with the excellencies of God's laws! How does he expatiate on their praises, both from their inherent qualities and admirable effects! (Ps xix 8–10, etc.).

There is a two-fold judgment of the understanding, the absolute and the comparative. The absolute judgment is when a man thinks such a course best in general, but not for him, or not under his present circumstances. Now, a godly man's judgment is for the ways of God, and that not only the absolute, but comparative judgment. He thinks them not only the best in general, but best for him. He looks upon the rules of religion not only as tolerable, but desirable; yea, more desirable than gold, fine gold; yea, much fine gold.

His judgment is fully determined that it is best to be holy, that it is best to be strict, that it is in itself the most eligible course, and that it is for him the wisest and most rational and desirable choice. Hear the godly man's judgment; '*I know, O Lord, that thy judgments are right; I love thy commandments above gold, yea,*

[46]

above fine gold; I esteem all thy precepts concerning all things to be right; and I hate every false way' (Ps cxix 127–128). Mark, he approves of all that God requires, and disapproves of all that He forbids. '*Righteous, O Lord, and upright are thy judgments. Thy testimonies that thou hast commanded are righteous and very faithful. Thy word is true from the beginning, and every one of thy righteous judgments endureth for ever*' (Ps cxix). See how readily and fully he subscribes; he declares his assent and consent to it, and all and every thing contained therein.

(ii) **The desire of the heart** is to know the whole mind of Christ. He would not have one sin undiscovered, nor be ignorant of one duty required. It is the natural and earnest breathing of a sanctified heart: 'Lord, if there be any way of wickedness in me, do Thou reveal it. What I know not, teach Thou me; and if I have done iniquity, I will do it no more.' The unsound convert is willingly ignorant, he does not love to come to the light. He is willing to keep such and such a sin, and therefore is loath to know it to be a sin, and will not let in the light at that window. Now, the gracious heart is willing to know the whole latitude and compass of his Maker's law. He receives with all acceptation the Word which convinces him of any duty that he knew not, or minded not before, or which uncovers any sin that lay hid before.

(iii) **The free and resolved choice of the will** is for the ways of Christ, before all the pleasures of sin and prosperities of the world. His consent is not extorted by some extremity of anguish, nor is it only a sudden and hasty resolve, but he is deliberately purposed, and comes freely to the choice. True, the flesh will rebel, yet the prevailing part of his will is for Christ's laws and government, so that he takes them up not as his toil or burden, but as his bliss. While the unsanctified goes in Christ's ways as in chains and fetters, the true convert does it heartily, and counts Christ's laws his liberty. He delights in the beauties of holiness, and has this inseparable mark. He had rather, if he might have his choice, live a strict and holy life, than the most prosperous and flourishing worldly life. '*There went with Saul a band of men*

[47]

whose hearts God had touched' (1 Sam x 26). When God touches the hearts of His chosen, they presently follow Christ, and, though drawn, do freely run after Him, and willingly devote themselves to the service of the Lord, seeking Him with their whole desire. Fear has its uses; but this is not the main-spring of motion with a sanctified heart. Christ does not control His subjects by force, but is King of a willing people. They are, through His grace, freely devoted to His service. They serve out of choice, not as slaves, but as the son or spouse, from a spring of love and a loyal mind. In a word, the laws of Christ are the convert's love, delight, and continual study.

(iv) **The bent of his course** is directed to keep God's statutes. It is the daily care of his life to walk with God. He seeks great things, he has noble designs, though he fall too short. He aims at nothing less than perfection; he desires it, he reaches after it; he would not rest in any degree of grace, till he were quite rid of sin, and perfected in holiness (Phil iii 11–14).

Here the hypocrite's rottenness may be discovered. He desires holiness, as one well said, only as a bridge to heaven, and inquires earnestly what is the least that will serve his turn; and if he can get but so much as may bring him to heaven, this is all he cares for. But the sound convert desires holiness for holiness' sake, and not merely for heaven's sake. He would not be satisfied with so much as might save him from hell, but desires the highest degree. Yet desires are not enough. What is your way and your course? Are the drift and scope of your life altered? Is holiness your pursuit, and religion your business? If not, you fall short of sound conversion.

And is this which we have described, the conversion that is of absolute necessity to salvation? Then be informed, that strait is the gate and narrow is the way that leadeth unto life – that there are few that find it – that there is need of divine power savingly to convert a sinner to Jesus Christ.

Again, be exhorted, O man, to examine yourself. What does conscience say? Does it begin to accuse? Does it not pierce you as you go? Is this your judgment, and this your choice, and this your way, that we have described? If so, then it is well. But does your heart condemn you, and tell you of a certain sin you are living in against your conscience? Does it not tell you there is such and such a secret way of wickedness that you wish to pursue; such and such a duty that you make no conscience of?

Does not conscience carry you to your closet, and tell you how seldom prayer and reading are performed there? Does it not carry you to your family, and show you the charge of God, and the souls of your children that are neglected there? Does not conscience lead you to your shop, your trade, and tell you of some iniquity there? Does it not carry you to the public-house, or the private club, and blame you for the loose company you keep there, the precious time which you mis-spend there, the talents which you waste there? Does it not carry you into your secret chamber, and read there your condemnation?

O conscience! do your duty. In the name of the living God, I command you, discharge your office. Lay hold upon this sinner, fall upon him, arrest him, apprehend him, undeceive him. What! will you flatter and soothe him while he lives in his sins? Awake, O conscience! What meanest thou, O sleeper? What! have you no reproof in your mouth? What! shall this soul die in his careless neglect of God and of eternity, and you altogether hold your peace? What! shall he go on still in his trespasses, and yet have peace? Oh, rouse yourself, and do your work. Now let the preacher in your bosom speak. Cry aloud, and spare not; lift up thy voice like a trumpet. Let not the blood of his soul be required at your hands.

3

The necessity of conversion

It may be you are ready to say, 'What does this stir mean?' and are apt to wonder why I follow you with such earnestness, still ringing the same lesson in your ears, that you should repent and be converted. But I must say to you, as Ruth to Naomi, '*Entreat me not to leave thee, or to return from following after thee.*' Were it a matter of indifference, might you be saved as you are, I would gladly let you alone; but would you not have me concerned for you, when I see you ready to perish? As the Lord liveth, before whom I am, I have not the least hope of seeing your face in heaven, except you be converted. I utterly despair of your salvation, except you will be prevailed with thoroughly to turn and give up yourself to God in holiness and newness of life. Has God said, *Except a man be born again he cannot see the kingdom of God*', and yet do you wonder why your ministers labour so earnestly for you? Do not think it strange that I am earnest with you to follow after holiness, and long to see the image of God upon you. Never did any, nor shall any, enter into heaven by any other way but this. The conversion described is not a high attainment of some advanced Christians, but every soul that is saved undergoes this change.

It was a saying of the noble Roman when he was hasting with corn to the city in the famine and the mariners were loath to set sail in foul weather, 'It is necessary for us to sail – it is not necessary for us to live.' What is it that you count necessary? Is your bread necessary? Is your breath necessary? Then your conversion is much more necessary. Indeed, this is the one thing necessary. Your possessions are not necessary; you may sell all for the pearl of great price, and yet be a gainer by the purchase. Your life is not necessary; you may part with it for Christ, to infinite advantage. Your reputation is not necessary; you may be reproached for the name of Christ, and yet be happy; yes, you may be much more happy in reproach than in repute. But your conversion is necessary; your salvation depends upon it; and is it not needful in so important a matter to take care? On this one point depends your making or marring to all eternity.

But I shall more particularly show the necessity of conversion in five things.

1: Without conversion your being is in vain.

Is it not a pity you should be good for nothing, an unprofitable burden of the earth, a mere wart in the body of the universe? Thus you are, while unconverted, for you cannot answer the end of your being. Is it not for the divine pleasure that you are and were created? Did not God make you for Himself? Are you a man, and have you reason? Then, think how you came into being and why you exist. Behold God's workmanship in your body, and ask yourself for what purpose did God rear this fabric? Consider the noble faculties of your heaven-born soul. To what end did God bestow these excellencies? Was it to no other end than that you should please yourself, and gratify your senses? Did God send men into the world, only like the swallows, to gather a few sticks and mud, and build their nests, and rear up their young, and then away? The very heathen could see farther than this. Are you so *fearfully and wonderfully made*', and do you not yet reason with yourself – surely, it was for some noble and exalted end?

O man! set your reason a little in the chair. Is it not a pity such a goodly fabric should be raised in vain? Verily you are in vain, except you are for God. It were better you had no being than not be for Him. Would you serve your end? You must repent and be converted; without this you are to no purpose; indeed, to bad purpose.

You are to no purpose. Unconverted man is like a choice instrument that has every string broken or out of tune. The Spirit of the living God must repair and tune it by the grace of regeneration, and sweetly move it by the power of actuating grace, or else your prayers will be but howlings, and all your service will make no music in the ears of the Most Holy. All your powers and faculties are so corrupt in your natural state that, except you be purged from dead works, you cannot serve the living God. An unsanctified man cannot work the work of God.

[1] He has no skill in it. He is altogether as unskilful in the work as in the word of righteousness. There are great mysteries in the practice as well as in the principles of godliness. Now the unregenerate do not know the mysteries of the kingdom of heaven. You may as well expect him to read that never learned the alphabet, or look for goodly music on the lute from one that never set his hand to an instrument, as that a natural man should do the Lord any pleasing service. He must first be taught of God (Jn vi 45), taught to pray (Lk xi 1), taught to profit (Is xlviii 17), taught to go (Hos xi 3), or else he will be utterly at a loss.

[2] He has no strength for it. How weak is his heart! (Ezek xvi 30). He is soon tired. The Sabbath, what a weariness is it! (Mal. i 13). He is without strength (Rom v 6), yea, dead in sin (Eph ii 5).

[3] He has no mind to it. He desires not the knowledge of God's ways (Job xxi 14). He does not know them, and he does not care to know them (Ps lxxxii 5). He knows not, neither will he understand.

[4] He has neither due instruments nor materials for it. A man may as well hew the marble without tools, or paint without colours or brushes, or build without materials, as perform any acceptable service without the graces of the Spirit, which are both the materials and instruments in the work. Almsgiving is not a service of God but of vain-glory, if it does not spring from love to God. What is the prayer of the lips without grace in the heart, but the carcase without life? What are all our confessions, unless

they are exercises of godly sorrow and unfeigned repentance? What are our petitions, unless animated with holy desires and faith in the attributes and promises of God? What are our praises and thanksgiving, unless they spring from the love of God, and a holy gratitude and sense of God's mercies in the heart? So that a man may as well expect that trees should speak, or look for motion from the dead, as look for any service, holy and acceptable to God, from the unconverted. When the tree is evil, how can the fruit be good?

Also, without conversion you live to bad purpose. The unconverted soul is a very cage of unclean birds (Rev xviii 2), a sepulchre full of corruption and rottenness (Mt xxiii 27), a loathsome carcase full of crawling worms, and sending forth a most noxious stench in the nostrils of God (Ps xiv 3). O dreadful case! Do you not yet see a change to be needful? Would it not have grieved one to see the golden consecrated vessels of God's temple turned into quaffing bowls of drunkenness, and polluted with the idol's service? (Dan v 2-3). Was it such an abomination to the Jews when Antiochus set up the picture of a swine at the entrance of the temple? How much more abominable, then, would it have been to have had the very temple itself turned into a stable or a sty; and to have had the holy of holies served like the house of Baal! This is just the case of the unregenerate. All your members are turned into instruments of unrighteousness, servants of Satan, and your inmost heart into a receptacle of uncleanness. You may see what kind of guests are within by what come out; for, 'out of the heart proceed evil thoughts, murders, adulteries, fornications, thefts, false witness, blasphemies' (Mt xv 19). This black troop shows what a hell there is within.

O abuse insufferable! to see a heaven-born soul abased to such vileness; to see the glory of God's creation, the chief of the works of God, the lord of this lower world, eating husks with the prodigal! Was it such a lamentation to see those that did feed delicately sit desolate in the streets; and the precious sons of Zion, comparable to fine gold, esteemed as earthen pitchers; and those that were clothed in scarlet embrace dunghills? (Lam iv 2, 5). And is it not much more fearful to see the only being that has immortality in this lower world and carries the stamp of God, become as a vessel wherein is no pleasure, and be put to the most sordid use? O indignity intolerable! Better you were dashed in a thousand pieces, than continue to be abased to so vile a service.

2: Not only man, but **the whole visible creation is in vain without conversion.** God has made all the visible creatures in heaven and earth for the service of man, and man only is the spokesman for all the rest. Man is, in the world, like the tongue to the body, which speaks for all the members. The other creatures cannot praise their Maker, except by dumb signs and hints to man that he should speak for them. Man is, as it were, the high priest of God's creation, to offer the sacrifice of praise for all his fellow-creatures. The Lord God expects a tribute of praise from all His works. Now, all the rest do bring in their tribute to man, and pay it by his hand. So then, if a man is false, and faithless, and selfish, God is robbed of all, and has no active glory from His works.

O dreadful thought! that God should build such a world as this, and lay out such infinite power, and wisdom, and goodness thereupon, and all in vain; and that man should be guilty, at last, of robbing and spoiling Him of the glory of all! O think of this. While you are unconverted, all the offices of the creatures are in vain to you. Your food nourishes you in vain. The sun holds forth its light to you in vain. Your clothes warm you in vain. Your beast carries you in vain. In a word, the unwearied labour and continued travail of the whole creation, as to you, are in vain. The service of all the creatures that drudge for you, and yield forth their strength unto you, with which you should serve their Maker, is all but lost labour. Hence, '*the whole creation groaneth*' (Rom viii 22) under the abuse of unsanctified men who pervert all things to the service of their lusts, quite contrary to the very end of their being.

[54]

3: Without conversion your religion is vain. All your religious performances will be but lost; for they can neither please God nor save your soul, which are the very ends of religion (Rom viii 8; 1 Cor xiii 2–3). Be your services ever so specious, yet God has no pleasure in them (Is i 14; Mal i 10). Is not that man's case dreadful whose sacrifices are as murders, and whose prayers are a breath of abomination? (Is lxvi 3; Prov xxviii 9). Many under conviction think they will set upon mending, and that a few prayers and alms will set all right again; but alas, sirs, while your hearts remain unsanctified your duties will not pass. How punctilious was Jehu! and yet all was rejected because his heart was not upright (2 Kgs x with Hos i 4). How blameless was Paul! and yet, being unconverted, all was but loss (Phil iii 6–7). Men think they do much in attending to God's service, and are ready to set Him down so much their debtor; whereas their persons being unsanctified, their duties cannot be accepted.

O soul! do not think when your sins pursue you, that a little praying and reforming your ways will pacify God. You must begin with your heart. If that is not renewed, you can no more please God than one who, having unspeakably offended you, should bring you the most loathsome thing to pacify you; or having fallen into the mire, should think with his filthy embraces to reconcile you.

It is a great misery to labour in the fire. The poets could not invent a worse hell for Sisyphus than to be ever toiling to get the stone up the hill, and then that it should presently roll down again and renew his labour. God threatens it as the greatest temporal judgments, that they should build and not inhabit, plant and not gather, and that their labours should be eaten up by strangers (Deut xxviii 30, 38–41). Is it so great a misery to lose our common labours, to sow in vain, and to build in vain? How much more to lose our pains in religion – to pray, and hear, and fast in vain! This is an undoing and eternal loss. Be not deceived; if you go on in your sinful state, though you should spread forth your hands, God will hide His eyes; though you make many prayers, He will not hear (Is i 15). If a man without skill set about our work, and spoil it in the doing, though he take much pains, we give him but small thanks. God will be worshipped after the due order. If a servant do our work, but quite contrary to our order, he shall have stripes rather than praise. God's work must be done according to God's mind, or He will not be pleased; and this cannot be, except it be done with a holy heart.

4: Without true conversion your hopes are in vain. '*The hope of the hypocrite shall perish*' (Job viii 12–13). '*The Lord hath rejected thy confidences*' (Jer ii 37).

[1] The hope of comfort here is vain. It is not only necessary for the safety, but comfort of your condition, that you be converted. Without this, you shall not know peace (Is lix 8). Without the fear of God you cannot have the comfort of the Holy Ghost (Acts ix 31). God speaks peace only to His people and to His saints (Ps lxxxv 8). If you have a false peace continuing in your sins, it is not of God's speaking, and therefore you may guess the author. Sin is a real sickness (Is i 5), yea, the worst of sickness; it is a leprosy in the head (Lev xiii 44); the plague in the heart (1 Kgs viii 38); it is brokenness in the bones (Ps li 8); it pierces, it wounds, it racks, it torments (1 Tim vi 10). A man may as well expect ease when his diseases are in their full strength, or his bones out of joint, as true comfort while in his sins.

O wretched man, that can have no ease in this case but what comes from the deadliness of the disease! You shall have the poor sick man saying in his wildness, he is well; when you see death in his face, he would be up and about his business, when the very next step is likely to be to his grave. The unsanctified often see nothing amiss; they think themselves whole, and cry not for the physician; but this only shows the danger of their case.

Sin naturally breeds diseases and disturbances in the soul. What a continual tempest is there in a discontented mind! What a corroding evil is inordinate care! What is passion but a very fever in the mind? What is lust but a fire in the bones? What is pride but a deadly dropsy? or covetousness but an insatiable and insufferable thirst? or malice and envy but venom in the very heart? Spiritual sloth is but a scurvy in the mind, and carnal security a mortal lethargy. How can that soul have true comfort which is under so many diseases? But converting grace cures, and so eases the mind, and prepares the soul for a settled, standing, immortal peace. '*Great peace have they that love thy law, and nothing shall offend them*' (Ps cxix 165). They are the ways of wisdom that afford pleasure and peace (Prov iii 17). David had infinitely more pleasure in the Word than in all the delights of his court (Ps cxix 103, 127). The conscience cannot be truly pacified until soundly purified (Heb x 22). Cursed is that peace which is maintained in a way of sin (Deut xxix 19–20). Two sorts of peace are more to be dreaded than all the troubles in the world: peace with sin, and peace in sin.

[2] The hope of salvation hereafter is in vain. This hope is most injurious to God, most pernicious to yourself. There is death, despair, and blasphemy in this hope.

There is death in it. Your confidence shall be rooted out of your tabernacles, God will up with it root and branch; it will bring you to the king of terrors (Job xviii 14). Though you may lean upon this house, it will not stand, but will prove like a ruinous building which, when a man trusts to it, falls down about him (Job viii 15).

There is despair in it. '*Where is the hope of the hypocrite when God taketh away his soul?*' (Job xxvii 8). Then there is an end for ever of his hope. Indeed, the hope of the righteous has an end, but it is not a destructive, but a perfective end. His hope ends in fruition, others in frustration. The godly may say at death, 'It is finished'; but the wicked, 'It is perished', and may earnestly bemoan himself, as Job did, though mistakenly, in his case, '*Where now is my hope? He hath destroyed me; I am gone, and my hope is removed like a tree*' (Job xix 10). '*The righteous hath hope in his death*' (Prov xiv 32). When nature is dying, his hopes are living; when his body is languishing, his hopes are flourishing; his hope is a living hope, but others a dying, yea, a damning, soul-undoing hope. '*When a wicked man dieth, his expectation shall perish; and the hope of unjust men perisheth*' (Prov xi 7). It shall be cut off and prove like a spider's web (Job viii 14) which he spins out of his own bowels; but then comes death and destroys all, and so there is an eternal end of his confidence in which he trusted. '*The eyes of the wicked shall fail and their hope shall be as the giving up of the ghost*' (Job xi 20). Wicked men are fixed in their carnal hope, and will not be beaten out of it; they hold it fast, they will not let it go, but death will knock off their fingers. Though we cannot undeceive them, death and judgment will. When death strikes his dart through your liver, it will ruin your soul and your hopes together. The unsanctified have hope only in this life, and therefore are of all men most miserable. When death comes, it lets them out into the amazing gulf of endless despair.

There is blasphemy in it. To hope we shall be saved, though continuing unconverted, is to hope that we shall prove God a liar. He has told you that, merciful and compassionate as He is, He will never save you notwithstanding, if you go on in a course of ignorance or unrighteousness. In a word, He has told you that whatever you are or do, nothing shall avail you to salvation unless you become new creatures. Now, to say God is merciful and to hope that He will save us without conversion, is in effect to say, 'We hope that God will not do as He says.' We must not set God's attributes at variance. God has resolved to glorify His mercy, but not to the prejudice of His truth, as the presumptuous sinner will find to his everlasting sorrow.

Objection: But we hope in Jesus Christ, we put our whole trust in God, and therefore do not doubt that we shall be saved.

Answer: This is not hope in Christ, but hope against Christ. To hope to see the kingdom of God without being born again, to hope to find eternal life in the broad way, is to hope Christ will prove a false prophet. David's plea is, '*I hope in thy word*' (Ps cxix 81). But this hope is against God's Word. Show me a word of Christ for your hope that He will save you in your ignorance or profane neglect of His service, and I will never try to shake your confidence.

God rejects this hope with abhorrence. Those condemned by the prophet went on in their sins; yet, says the prophet, *'will they lean upon the Lord'* (Mic iii 11). God will not endure to be made a prop to men in their sins. The Lord rejected those presumptuous sinners that went on still in their trespasses and yet would stay themselves on Israel's God, as a man would shake off the briers that cleave to his garment.

If your hope is worth anything, it will purify you from your sins (1 Jn iii 3), but cursed is that hope which cherishes men in their sins.

Objection: Would you have us despair?

Answer: You must despair of ever coming to heaven as you are, that is, while unconverted. You must despair of ever seeing the face of God without holiness. But you must by no means despair of finding mercy upon your thorough repentance and conversion. Neither may you despair of attaining to repentauce and conversion in the use of God's means.

5: Without conversion all that Christ has done and suffered will be, as to you, in vain. That is, it will in no way avail you to salvation. Many urge this as a sufficient ground for their hope, that Christ died for sinners; but I must tell you, Christ never died to save impenitent and unconverted sinners, so continuing. A great divine was accustomed in his private dealings with souls to ask two questions. What has Christ done for you? What has Christ wrought in you? Without the application of the Spirit in regeneration, we have no saving interest in the benefits of redemption. I tell you from the Lord, that Christ Himself cannot save you if you go on in this state.

[1] To save men in their sins would be against His trust. The Mediator is the servant of the Father, shows His commission from Him, acts in His name, and pleads His command for His

justification (Jn x 18, 36; Jn vi 38, 40). God has committed all things to Him, entrusted His own glory and the salvation of His elect with Him (Mt xi 27; Jn xvii 2). Accordingly, Christ gives His Father an account of both parts of His trust before He leaves the world (Jn xvii). Now Christ would quite thwart His Father's glory, tarnish His greatest trust, if He should save men in their sins: for this would overturn all His counsels, and offer violence to all His attributes.

It would overturn all God's counsels, of which this is the order, that men should be brought to salvation through sanctification (2 Thess ii 13). He has chosen them that they should be holy (Eph i 4). They are elected to pardon and life through sanctification (1 Pet i 2). If you can repeal the law of God's immutable counsel, or corrupt Him whom the Father has sealed to go directly against His commission, then, and not otherwise, you may get to heaven in this condition. To hope that Christ will save you while unconverted, is to hope that Christ will prove false to His trust. He never did, nor ever will save one soul but whom the Father has given Him in election, and drawn to Him in effectual calling (Jn vi 37, 44). Be assured, Christ will save none in a way contrary to His Father's will.

To save men in their sins would offer violence to all the attributes of God.

To His *justice*. The righteousness of God's judgment lies in rendering to all according to their works. Now, should men sow to the flesh, and yet of the Spirit reap everlasting life, where were the glory of divine justice, since it would be given to the wicked according to the work of the righteous?

To His *holiness*. If God should not only save sinners, but save them in their sins, His most pure and strict holiness would be exceedingly defaced. The unsanctified, in the eyes of God's holiness, are worse than a swine or viper. It would be offering the extremest violence to the infinite purity of the divine nature to have such dwell with Him. They cannot stand in His judgment: they cannot abide His presence. If holy David would not endure such in his house, no, nor in his sight (Ps ci 3, 7), can we think God will? Should He take men as they are, from the mire of their filthiness to the glory of heaven, the world would think that God was at no such great distance from sin, nor had any such dislike to it as we are told He has. They would be ready to conclude that God was altogether such an one as themselves, as some of old wickedly did, from the forbearance of God (Ps l 21).

To His *veracity*. God has declared from heaven that if any say he shall have peace, though he should go on in the imagination of his heart, His wrath shall smoke against that man (Deut. xxix 19–20). He has declared that they only that confess and forsake their sins shall find mercy (Prov xxviii 13). He has declared that they that shall enter into His hill must be of clean hands and a pure heart (Ps xxiv 3, 4). Where were God's truth if, notwithstanding all this, He should bring men to salvation without conversion? O desperate sinner, that dares to hope that Christ will make His Father a liar and nullify His word to save you!

To His *wisdom*. This were to throw away the choicest of mercies on them that would not value them, nor were any way suited to them.

They would not value them. The unsanctified sinner puts but little price upon God's great salvation. He thinks no more of Christ than they that are whole do of the physician. He prizes not His balm, values not His cure, but tramples on His blood. Now, would it stand with wisdom to force pardon and life upon those that would return no thanks for them? Will the all-wise God, when He has forbidden us to do it, throw His holy things to dogs and His pearls to swine, that would, as it were, but turn again and rend Him? This would make mercy to be despised indeed. Wisdom requires that life be given in a way suitable to God's honour, and that God provide for the securing of His own glory as well as man's felicity. It would be dishonourable to God to bestow His choicest riches on them that have more pleasure in their sins than in the heavenly delights that He offers. God would lose the praise and glory of His grace, if He should cast it away upon them that were not only unworthy but unwilling.

Also, the mercies of God are no way suited to the unconverted. God's wisdom is seen in suiting things to each other, the means to the end, the object to the faculty, the quality of the gift to the capacity of the receiver. Now, if Christ should bring the unregenerate sinner to heaven, he could take no more felicity there than a beast would, if you should bring him into a beautiful room to the society of learned men; whereas the poor thing had much rather be grazing with his fellows in the field. Alas, what could an unsanctified man do in heaven? He could not be content there because nothing suits him. The place does not suit him; he would be quite out of his element, a fish out of water. The company does not suit him; what communion has darkness with light? corruption with perfection? vileness and sin with glory and immortality? The employment does not suit him; the anthems of heaven do not fit his mouth, do not suit his ear. Can you charm a donkey with music; or will you bring him to your organ and expect that he should make melody, or keep time with the tuneful choir? Had he skill, he would have no will, and so could find no pleasure in it. Spread your table with delicacies before a languishing patient, and it will be but an offence. Alas, if the poor man think a sermon long and say of a Sabbath-day, 'What a weariness is it!' how miserable would he think it to be engaged in an everlasting Sabbath!

To His *immutability*, or else to His omniscience or omnipotence. It is enacted in heaven, and enrolled in the decree of the court above, that none but the pure in heart shall see God (Mt v 8). Now, if Christ bring any to heaven unconverted, either He must get them in without His Father's knowledge, and then where is His omniscience? or against His will, and then where were His omnipotence? or He must change His will, and then where were His immutability?

Sinner, will you not give up your vain hope of being saved in this condition? Bildad says, '*Shall the earth be forsaken for thee;*

or the rocks be moved out of their place?' (Job xviii 4). May I not much more reason with you? Shall the laws of heaven be reversed for you? Shall the everlasting foundations be overturned for you? Shall Christ put out the eye of His Father's omniscience, or shorten the arm of His eternal power for you? Shall divine justice be violated for you; or the brightness of His holiness be blemished for you? O the impossibility, absurdity, blasphemy, of such a confidence! To think Christ will ever save you in this condition is to make the Saviour become a sinner, and do more wrong to the infinite Majesty than all the wicked on earth or devils in hell ever did, or ever could do; and yet will you not give up such a blasphemous hope?

[2] To save men in their sins would be against the word of Christ. We need not say, '*Who shall ascend into heaven, to bring down Christ from above? Or, who shall descend into the deep, to bring up Christ from beneath? The word is nigh us*' (Rom x 6–8). Are you agreed that Christ shall end the controversy? Hear then His own words: '*Except ye be converted, ye shall in no wise enter into the kingdom of heaven.*' '*Ye must be born again.*' '*If I wash thee not, thou hast no part in me.*' '*Except ye repent ye shall perish*' (Mt xviii 3; Jn iii 7; Jn xiii 8; Lk xiii 3). One word, one would think, were enough from Christ; but how often and earnestly does He reiterate it: '*Verily, verily, except a man be born again, he shall not see the kingdom of God*' (Jn iii 3). Yea, He not only asserts but proves the necessity of the new birth from the fleshliness and sinfulness of man from his first birth, by reason of which man is no more fit for heaven than the beast is for the chamber of the king. And will you yet rest in your own presumptuous confidence, directly against Christ's words? He must go quite against the law of His kingdom and rule of His judgment, to save you in this state.

[3] To save men in their sins would be against the oath of Christ. He has lifted up His hand to heaven, He has sworn that those who remain in unbelief and know not His ways (that is, are ignorant of them, or disobedient to them) shall not enter into His

rest (Heb iii 18). And will you not yet believe, O sinner, that He is earnest? The covenant of grace is confirmed by an oath and sealed by blood; but all must be made void, and another way to heaven found out if you be saved, living and dying unsanctified. God is come to His last terms with man, and has condescended as far as in honour He could. Men cannot be saved while unconverted, except they could get another covenant made, and the whole frame of the Gospel, which was established for ever with such dreadful solemnities, quite altered. And must not they be demented who hope that they shall?

[4] To save men in their sins would be against His honour. God will so show His love to the sinner as at the same time to show His hatred to sin. Therefore, he that names the name of Jesus must depart from iniquity and deny all ungodliness; and he that has hope of life by Christ must purify himself as He is pure, otherwise Christ would be thought a favourer of sin (2 Tim ii 19; Tit ii 12; 1 Jn iii 3). The Lord Jesus would have all the world know, that though He pardons sin, He will not protect it. If holy David say, '*Depart from me, all ye workers of iniquity*' (Ps vi 8), and shut the doors against them (Ps ci 7), shall we not much more expect it from Christ's holiness? Would it be for His honour, to have the dogs to the table, or to lodge the swine with His children, or to have Abraham's bosom to be a nest of vipers?

[5] To save men in their sins would be against His offices. God has exalted Him to be a Prince and a Saviour (Acts v 31). He would act against both, should He save men in their sins. It is the office of a king to be a terror to evil-doers, and a praise to them that do well. '*He is a minister of God, a revenger to execute wrath on him that doeth evil*' (Rom xiii 4). Now, should Christ favour the ungodly, so continuing, and take those to reign with Him that would not that He should reign over them, this would be quite against His office. He therefore reigns that He may put His enemies under His feet. Now, should He lay them in His bosom, He would frustrate the end of His regal power; it belongs to

Christ, as a King, to subdue the hearts and slay the lusts of His chosen (Ps xlv 5; Ps cx 3). What king would take rebels in open hostility into his court? What were this but to betray life, kingdom, government, and all together? If Christ is a King, He must have honour, homage, subjection. Now, to save men while in their natural enmity, were to obscure His dignity, lose His authority, bring contempt on His government, and sell His dear-bought rights for naught.

Again, as Christ would not be a Prince, so neither a Saviour, if He should do this; for His salvation is spiritual. He is called Jesus because He saves His people *from* their sins (Mt i 21). So that, should He save them *in* their sins, He would be neither Lord nor Jesus. To save men from the punishment, and not from the power of sin, were to do His work by halves, and be an imperfect Saviour. His office as the Deliverer is to turn ungodliness from Jacob (Rom xi 26). He is sent to bless men, in turning them from their iniquities (Acts iii 26), to make an end of sin (Dan ix 24). So that He would destroy His own designs, and nullify His offices, to save men in their unconverted state.

Arise then! What meanest thou, O sleeper? Awake, O secure sinner, lest you be consumed in your iniquities: say, as the lepers, '*If we sit here, we shall die*' (2 Kgs vii 3–4). Verily, it is not more certain that you are now out of hell than that you shall speedily be in it, except you repent and be converted. There is but this one door for you to escape by. Arise then, O sluggard, and shake off your excuses; how long will you slumber and fold your hands to sleep? Will you lie down in the midst of the sea, or sleep on the top of a mast? (Prov xxiii 34). There is no remedy, but you must either turn or burn. There is an unchangeable necessity of the change of your condition, unless you have resolved to abide the worst of it, and try it out with the Almighty. If you love your life, O man, arise and come away. I think I see the Lord Jesus laying the merciful hands of a holy violence upon you; I think He acts like the angels to Lot: '*Then the angels hastened Lot, saying, Arise, lest thou be consumed. And, while he lingered, the*

men laid hold upon his hand, the Lord being merciful unto him;
and they brought him without the city, and said, Escape for thy
life, stay not in all the plain; escape to the mountains, lest thou be
consumed' (Gen xix 15-17).

O how wilful will your destruction be if you should yet harden
yourself in your sinful state! But none of you can say that you
have not had fair warning. Yet I cannot leave you so. It is not
enough for me to have delivered my own soul. What! shall I go
away without my errand? Will none of you arise and follow me?
Have I been all this while speaking to the wind? Have I been
charming the deaf adder, or allaying the restless ocean with argument? Do I speak to the trees and rocks, or to men? to the tombs
and monuments of the dead, or to the living? If you are men and
not senseless stocks, stop and consider where you are going!
If you have the reason and understanding of men, do not dare
to run into the flames, and fall into hell with your eyes open; but
stop and think, and set about the work of repentance. What,
men? and yet run into the pit, when the very beasts will not be
forced in? What, endowed with reason? and yet trifle with death
and hell, and the vengeance of the Almighty? Are men only
distinguished from brutes in that these, having no foresight, have
no care to provide for the things to come, and will you, who are
warned, not hasten your escape from eternal torments? O show
yourselves men, and let reason prevail with you.

Is it a reasonable thing for you to contend against the Lord
your Maker, or to harden yourselves against His word, as though
the Strength of Israel would lie? (Is xlv 9; Job ix 4; 1 Sam xv 29).
Is it reasonable that an understanding creature should lose, yea,
live quite against the very end of his being? Is it reasonable that
the only being in this world that God has made capable of
knowing His will and bringing Him glory, should yet live in
ignorance of his Maker, and be unserviceable to His use, yea,
should be engaged against Him, and spit his venom in the face
of his Creator? Hear, O heavens, and give ear, O earth, and let
the creatures without sense judge if this be reason, that man whom

God has nourished and brought up, should rebel against Him? Judge in your own selves. Is it a reasonable undertaking for briers and thorns to set themselves in battle against the devouring fire? or for the potsherd of the earth to strive with its Maker? You will say, 'This is not reason'; or surely the eye of reason is quite put out. And, if this be not reason, then there is no reason that you should continue as you are, but there is every reason in the world that you should immediately turn and repent.

What shall I say? I could spend myself in this argument. O that you would only hearken to me; that you would now set upon a new course! Will you not be made clean? When shall it once be? Reader, will you sit down and consider the fore-mentioned argument, and debate it whether it be not best to turn? Come, and let us reason together. Is it good for you to be here? Is it good for you to try whether God will be as good as His word, and to harden yourself in a conceit that all is well with you while you remain unsanctified?

Alas, for such sinners! must they perish at last by hundreds? What course shall I use with them that I have not tried? *'What shall I do for the daughter of my people?'* (Jer ix 7).

'O Lord God, help. Alas, shall I leave them thus? If they will not hear me, yet do Thou hear me. O that they might live in Thy sight! Lord, save them, or they perish. My heart would melt to see their houses on fire when they were fast asleep in their beds; and shall not my soul be moved within me to see them falling into endless perdition? Lord, have compassion, and save them out of the burning. Put forth Thy divine power, and the work will be done.'

4

The marks of the unconverted

While we keep aloof in general statements there is little fruit to be expected; it is the hand-fight that does execution. David is not awakened by the prophet's hovering at a distance in parabolical insinuations. Nathan is forced to close with him, and tell him plainly, '*Thou art the man.*' Few will, in words, deny the necessity of the new birth; but they have a self-deluding confidence that the work is not to be done now. And because they know themselves to be free from that gross hypocrisy which takes up religion merely for a colour to deceive others, and for covering wicked designs, they are confident of their sincerity, and do not suspect that more close hypocrisy, in which the greatest danger lies and by which a man deceives his own soul. But man's deceitful heart is such a matchless cheat, and self-delusion so reigning and so fatal a disease, that I do not know which is the greater, the difficulty or the necessity of the undeceiving work that I am now upon. Alas for the unconverted, they must be undeceived, or they will be undone! But how shall this be effected?

'*Help, O all-searching Light, and let Thy discerning eye disclose the rotten foundation of the self-deceiver. Lead me, O Lord God, as Thou didst the prophet, into the chambers of imagery, and dig through the wall of sinners' hearts, and reveal the hidden abominations that are lurking out of sight in the dark. O send Thy angel before me to open the sundry wards of their hearts, as Thou didst before Peter, and make even the iron gates fly open of their own accord. And as Jonathan no sooner tasted the honey but his eyes were enlightened, so grant, O Lord, that when the poor deceived souls with whom I have to do shall cast their eyes upon these lines, their minds may be illuminated, and their consciences convinced and awakened, that they may see with their eyes, and hear with their ears, and be converted, and Thou mayest heal them.'*

This must be premised before we proceed, that it is most certain that men may have a confident persuasion that their hearts and states are good while yet they are unsound. Hear the Truth Himself who shows, in Laodicea's case, that men may be wretched, and miserable, and poor, and blind, and naked, and yet not know it; yes, they may be confident they are rich, and increased in grace (Rev iii 17). *'There is a generation that are pure in their own eyes, and yet are not washed from their filthiness'* (Prov xxx 12). Who better persuaded of his state than Paul, while he yet remained unconverted? (Rom vii 9). So that they are miserably deceived who take a strong confidence for a sufficient evidence. They that have no better proof than barely a strong persuasion that they are converted, are certainly as yet strangers to conversion.

But to come closer. As it was said to the adherents of Antichrist, so here; some of the unconverted carry their marks in their forehead more openly, and some in their hands more covertly. The apostle reckons up some upon whom he writes the sentence of death, as in these dreadful catalogues which I beseech you to attend to with all diligence: *'For this ye know, that no whoremonger, nor unclean person, nor covetous man, who is an idolater, hath any inheritance in the kingdom of Christ and of God. Let no man deceive you with vain words; for because of these things cometh the wrath of God upon the children of disobedience'* (Eph v 5–6). *'But the fearful, and unbelieving, and abominable, and murderers, and whoremongers, and sorcerers, and idolaters, and all liars, shall have their part in the lake that burneth with fire and brimstone, which is the second death'* (Rev xxi 8). *'Know ye not that the unrighteous shall not inherit the kingdom of God? Be not deceived: neither fornicators, nor idolaters, nor adulterers, nor effeminate, nor abusers of themselves with mankind, nor thieves, nor covetous, nor drunkards, nor revilers, nor extortioners, shall inherit the kingdom of God'* (1 Cor vi 9–10). Woe to them that have their name written in this catalogue. Such may know, as certainly as if God had told them from heaven, that they are unsanctified, and under an impossibility of being saved in this condition.

There are then these several classes that, past all dispute, are unconverted; they carry their marks in their foreheads.

[1] **The unclean.** These are ever reckoned among the goats, and have their names, whoever else is left out, in all the fore-mentioned catalogues.

[2] **The covetous.** These are ever branded for idolaters, and the doors of the kingdom are shut against them by name.

[3] **Drunkards.** Not only such as drink away their reason, but withal, yea, above all, such as are too strong for strong drink. The Lord fills His mouth with woes against these, and declares them to have no inheritance in the kingdom of God (Is v 11, 12, 22; Gal v 21).

[4] **Liars.** The God that cannot lie has told them that there is no place for them in His kingdom, no entrance into His hill; but their portion is with the father of lies, whose children they are, in the lake of burnings (Rev xxi 8, 27; Jn viii 44; Prov vi 17).

[5] **Swearers.** The end of these, without deep and speedy repentance, is swift destruction, and most certain and unavoidable condemnation (Jas v 12; Zech v 1–3).

[6] **Railers and backbiters** that love to take up a reproach against their neighbour, and fling all the dirt they can in his face, or else wound him secretly behind his back (Ps xv 1, 3; 1 Cor v 11).

[7] **Thieves, extortioners,** oppressors, that grind the poor, or defraud their brethren when they have opportunity. These must know that God is the avenger of all such (1 Thess iv 6). Hear O ye false and purloining and wasteful servants; hear, O ye deceitful tradesmen, hear your sentence! God will certainly shut His door against you, and turn your treasures of unrighteousness into the treasures of wrath, and make your ill-gotten silver and

gold to torment you, like burning metal in your flesh (Jas v 2–3).

[8] **All that do ordinarily live in the profane neglect of God's worship,** that do not hear His Word, that do not call on His name, that restrain prayer before God, that do not mind their own nor their families' souls, but live without God in the world (Jn viii 47: Job xv 4; Ps xiv 4; Ps lxxix 6; Eph ii 12 and iv 18).

[9] **Frequenters and lovers of vain company.** God has declared that He will be the destroyer of all such, and that they shall never enter into the hill of His rest (Prov ix 6 and xiii 20).

[10] **Scoffers at religion,** that make a scorn of precise living, and mock at the messengers and diligent servants of the Lord, and at their holy profession, and make themselves merry with the weakness and failings of professing Christians. '*Hear, ye despisers,*' hear your dreadful doom (Prov xix 29; 2 Chron xxxvi 16).

Sinner, consider diligently whether you are not to be found in one of these ranks, for if this is the case, you are in the gall of bitterness and bond of iniquity; for all these do carry their marks in their foreheads, and are undoubtedly the sons of death. And if so, the Lord pity our poor congregations. O how small a number will remain when these ten sorts are left out.

Sirs, what efforts you make to keep up your confidence of your good state when God from heaven declares against you, and pronounces you in a state of damnation! I would reason with you, as God with them, '*How canst thou say, I am not polluted? See thy way in the valley; know what thou hast done*' (Jer ii 23). Man, is not your conscience aware of your tricks of deceit, of your secret sins, of your way of lying? Yea, are not your friends, your family, your neighbours, witnesses to your profane neglect of God's worship, to your covetous practices, to your envious and malicious behaviour? May they not point at you as you go, 'There goes a gaming prodigal; there goes a drunken Nabal, a companion of evil-doers; there goes a railer, or a scoffer, or a loose-liver!' Beloved, God has written it as with a sunbeam in the Book by which you must be judged, that these are not the

[71]

marks of His children, and that none such, except renewed by converting grace, shall ever escape the damnation of hell.

O that you would now be persuaded to repent and turn from all your transgressions, or else iniquity will be your ruin (Ezek xviii 30). Alas, for poor hardened sinners. Must I leave you at last where you are? Must I leave the drinker still at his bar? Must I leave the malicious still in his venom? However, you must know that you have been warned, and that I am clear of your blood; and whether men will hear, or whether they will forbear, I will leave these Scriptures with them, which will prove either as thunderbolts to awaken them, or as searing-irons to harden them. '*God shall wound the head of his enemies, and the hairy scalp of such an one as goeth on still in his trespasses.*' '*He that, being often reproved, hardeneth his neck, shall suddenly be destroyed, and that without remedy.*' '*Because I have called, and ye refused; I have stretched out my hand, and no man regarded, I will laugh at your calamity – when your destruction cometh as a whirlwind*' (Ps lxviii 21; Prov xxix 1; Prov i 24–27).

And now I imagine many will begin to bless themselves, and think all is well, because they cannot be reproached with these grosser evils. But I must tell you that there is another sort of unsanctified persons, who carry their mark not in their foreheads but more secretly and covertly. These frequently deceive themselves and others, and pass for good Christians, when they are all the while unsound at heart. Many pass undiscovered till death and judgment bring all to light. These self-deceivers seem to come even to heaven's gate with confidence of their admission, and yet are turned away at last (Mt vii 22). I beseech you deeply to lay to heart and firmly retain this awakening consideration, that multitudes perish by the hand of some secret sin, that is not only hidden from others, but from want of observing their own hearts, is hidden even from themselves. A man may be free from open pollutions, and yet die at last by the hand of some unobserved iniquity; and there are these twelve hidden sins, through which souls go down by numbers into the chambers of eternal death.

These you must search carefully for, and take them as black marks wherever they are found, revealing a graceless and unconverted state; and as you love your lives, read carefully with a holy jealousy of yourselves, lest you should be the persons concerned.

[1] **Gross wilful ignorance** (Hos iv 6). O how many poor souls does this sin kill in the dark, while they think verily they have good hearts, and are all set for heaven. This is the murderer that despatches thousands in a silent manner, when they suspect nothing, and do not see the hand that destroys them. You shall find, whatever excuses you make for ignorance, that it is a soul-ruining evil (Is xxvii 11; 2 Thess i 8; 2 Cor iv 3). Ah, would it not have grieved a man's heart to see that dreadful spectacle when the poor Protestants were shut up in a barn, and a butcher came, with his hands warmed in human blood, and led them one by one, blindfold, to a block where he slew them one after another, by scores, in cold blood? But how much more should your hearts bleed to think of the hundreds that ignorance destroys in secret and leads blindfold to the block. Beware that this is not your case. Make no plea for ignorance; if you spare that sin, know that it will not spare you; and would a man keep a murderer in his bosom?

[2] **Secret reserves in closing with Christ.** To forsake all for Christ, to hate father and mother, yea, a man's own life for Him, *'This is a hard saying'* (Lk xiv 26). Some will do much, but they will not have the religion that will save them. They never come to be entirely devoted to Christ, nor to be fully resigned to Him. They must have the sweet sin; they mean to do themselves no harm; they have secret exceptions for life, liberty, or estate. Many take Christ thus, and never consider His self-denying terms, nor count the cost; and this error in the foundation mars all, and ruins them forever (Lk xiv 28–33).

[3] **Formality in religion.** Many rest in the outside of religion and in the external performance of holy duties. And very often

this most effectually deceives men, and more certainly undoes them than open profaneness; as it was in the Pharisee's case. They hear, they fast, they pray, they give alms, and therefore will not believe but their case is good. Whereas, resting in the work done, and coming short of the heart-work and the inward power and vitality of religion, they fall at last into the burning, from the flattering hope and confident persuasion of their being all set on the way to heaven. Oh dreadful case, when a man's religion shall serve only to harden him, and effectually to delude and deceive his own soul!

[4] **The prevalence of wrong motives in holy duties.** This was the bane of the Pharisees. Oh how many a poor soul is undone by this, and drops into hell before he discerns his mistake! He performs his 'good duties' and so thinks all is well, but does not perceive that he is actuated by carnal motives all the while. It is too true that even with the really sanctified many carnal ends will often creep in; but they are the matter of their hatred and humiliation, and never come to be habitually prevalent with them, and bear the greatest sway. But when the main thing that ordinarily moves a man to religious duties is some carnal end – as to satisfy his conscience, to get the reputation of being religious, to be seen of men, to show his own gifts and talents, to avoid the reproach of being a profane and irreligious person, or the like – this reveals an unsound heart. Oh Christians, if you would avoid self-deceit, see that you mind not only your actions but your motives.

[5] **Trusting in their own righteousness.** This is a soul-ruining mischief. When men trust in their own righteousness they do indeed reject Christ's. Beloved, you had need be watchful on every hand, for not only your sins, but your duties may undo you. It may be you never thought of this; but so it is, that a man may as certainly perish by his seeming righteousness and supposed graces as by gross sins; and that is, when a man trusts to these as his righteousness before God, for satisfying His justice, appeasing His wrath, procuring His favour, and obtaining His pardon. This

is to put Christ out of office, and make a Saviour of our own duties and graces. Beware of this, O professing Christians; you are much in duties, but this one fly will spoil all the ointment. When you have done most and best, be sure to go out of yourselves to Christ; reckon your own righteousness as filthy rags (Phil iii 9; Is lxiv 6).

[6] **A secret enmity against the strictness of religion.** Many moral persons, punctilious in their formal devotions, have yet a bitter enmity against strictness and zeal, and hate the life and power of religion. They do not like this forwardness, nor that men should make such a stir in religion. They condemn the strictness of religion as singularity, indiscretion, and intemperate zeal, and with them a zealous preacher or fervent Christian is but a wild enthusiast. These men do not love holiness as holiness (for then they would love the height of holiness), and therefore are undoubtedly rotten at heart, whatever good opinion they have of themselves.

[7] **The resting in a certain degree of religion.** When they have so much as will save them, as they suppose, they look no farther, and so show themselves short of true grace, which always sets men aspiring to perfection (Phil iii 13; Prov iv 18).

[8] **The predominant love of the world.** This is the sure evidence of an unsanctified heart. '*If any man love the world, the love of the Father is not in him*' (1 Jn ii 15). But how often does this sin lurk under the fair cover of forward profession. Yea, such a power of deceit is there in this sin that many times, when everybody else can see the man's worldliness and covetousness, he cannot see it himself, but has so many excuses and pretences for his eagerness after the world, that he blinds his own eyes and perishes in his self-deceit. How many professing Christians are there with whom the world has more of their hearts and affections than Christ, '*who mind earthly things*', and thereby are evidently after the flesh, and likely to end in destruction (Rom viii 5; Phil iii 19). Yet ask these men, and they will tell you confidently they prize Christ above all; for they do not see their own earthly-mindedness

for want of a strict observance of the workings of their own hearts. Did they but carefully search, they would quickly find that their greatest satisfaction is in the world, and that their greatest care and main endeavour are to get and secure the world, which are the certain signs of an unconverted sinner. May the professing part of the world take earnest heed lest they perish by the hand of this sin unobserved. Men may be, and often are, kept off from Christ as effectually by the inordinate love of lawful comforts, as by the most unlawful courses.

[9] **Reigning malice and envy against those that disrespect them, and are injurious to them.** Oh how do many that seem to be religious, remember injuries and carry grudges, rendering evil for evil, loving to take revenge, wishing evil to them that wrong them. This is directly against the rule of the Gospel, the pattern of Christ, and the nature of God. Doubtless, where this evil is kept boiling in the heart, and is not hated, resisted, and mortified, but habitually prevails, that person is in the very gall of bitterness, and in a state of death (Mt xviii 32–35; 1 Jn iii 14–15).

[10] **Unmortified pride.** When men love the praise of men more than the praise of God, and set their hearts upon men's esteem, applause, and approbation, it is most certain that they are yet in their sins, and strangers to true conversion (Jn xii 43; Gal i 10). When men do not see nor complain nor groan under the pride of their own hearts, it is a sign they are stark dead in sin. Oh how secretly does this live and reign in many hearts, and they know it not, but are very strangers to themselves (Jn ix 40).

[11] **The prevailing love of pleasure.** This is a black mark. When men give the flesh the liberty that it craves and pamper and please it, and do not deny and restrain it; when their great delight is in gratifying their bellies and pleasing their senses; whatever appearances they may have of religion, all is unsound. A flesh-pleasing life cannot be pleasing to God. '*They that are Christ's have crucified the flesh*', and are careful to keep it under as their enemy (Gal v 24; 1 Cor ix 25–27).

[12] **Carnal security**, or a presumptuous confidence that their

condition is already good. Many cry, 'Peace and safety', when sudden destruction is coming upon them. This was that which kept the foolish virgins sleeping when they should have been working – upon their beds when they should have been at the markets. They did not perceive their lack of oil till the bridegroom was come; and while they went to buy, the door was shut. And oh that these foolish virgins had no successors! Where is the place, yea, where is the house almost, where these do not dwell? Men are willing to cherish in themselves, upon ever so slight grounds, a hope that their condition is good, and so are not concerned about a change, and by these means perish in their sins. Are you at peace? Show me upon what grounds your peace is maintained. Is it Scripture peace? Can you show the distinguishing marks of a sound believer? Can you evidence that you have something more than any hypocrite in the world ever had? If not, fear this peace more than any trouble; and know that a carnal peace commonly proves the most mortal enemy of the soul, and whilst it smiles and kisses and speaks fairly, it fatally smites, as it were, under the fifth rib.

By this time I think I hear my readers crying out, with the disciples, '*Who then shall be saved?*' Set out from our congregations all those ten ranks of the profane on the one hand, and then take out all these twelve classes of self-deceiving hypocrites on the other hand, and tell me whether it is not a remnant that shall be saved. How few will be the sheep that shall be left, when all these shall be separated and set among the goats. For my part, of all my numerous hearers, I have no hope to see any of them in heaven that are to be found among these twenty-two classes that are here mentioned, except by sound conversion they are brought into another condition.

And now, conscience, do your work. Speak out, and speak home to him that hears or reads these lines. If you find any of these marks upon him, you must pronounce him utterly unclean. Do not take a lie into your mouth. Do not speak peace to him to whom God speaks no peace. Do not let sense bribe you, or self-love or carnal prejudice blind you. I summon you from the court of heaven to come and give evidence. As you will answer it at your peril, give a true report of the state and case of him that reads this book. Conscience, will you altogether hold your peace at such a time as this? I adjure you by the living God that you tell the truth. Is the man converted, or is he not? Does he allow himself in any way of wickedness, or does he not? Does he truly love, and please, and prize, and delight in God above all things, or not? Come, give a definite answer.

How long shall this soul live in uncertainty? O conscience, bring in your verdict. Is this man a new man, or is he not? How do you find it? Has there passed a thorough and mighty change upon him, or not? When was the time, where was the place, or what were the means by which this thorough change of the new birth was wrought in his soul? Speak, conscience; or if you cannot tell the time and place, can you show Scripture evidence that the work is done? Has the man ever been taken off from his false foundation, from the false hopes and false peace in which once he trusted? Has he been deeply convinced of sin, and of his lost and undone condition, and brought out of himself, and off from his sins, to give himself up entirely to Jesus Christ? Or do you not find him to this day under the power of ignorance, or in the mire of worldliness? Have you not found upon him the gains of unrighteousness? Do you not find him a stranger to prayer, a neglecter of the Word, a lover of this present world? Do you not sometimes catch him in a lie? Do you not find his heart fermented with malice, or burning with lust, or going after his covetousness? Speak plainly to all the forementioned particulars. Can you acquit this man, this woman, from being in any of the twenty-two classes here described? If he is found in any of them, set him aside; his portion is not with the saints. He must be converted and made a new creature, or he cannot enter the kingdom of God.

Beloved, do not be your own betrayers. Do not deceive your own hearts, nor set your hands to your own ruin by a wilful blinding of yourselves. Set up a tribunal in your own breasts. Bring the Word and conscience together. '*To the law and to the testimony.*' Hear what the Word concludes of your state. Oh follow the search till you find how the case stands. Make a mistake here, and you perish. And, such is the treachery of the heart, the subtlety of the temper, and the deceitfulness of sin, all conspiring to flatter and deceive the poor soul; and so common and easy it is to make a mistake, that it is a thousand to one that you will be deceived, unless you are very careful and thorough and impartial in the inquiry into your spiritual condition. Oh therefore be diligent in your work; go to the bottom, search with candles; weigh yourself in the balance, come to the standard of the sanctuary; bring your coin to the touchstone. Satan is a master of deceit; he can draw to the life; he is perfect in the trade; there is nothing which he cannot imitate. You cannot wish for any grace, but he can fit you with a counterfeit. Be jealous; trust not even your own heart. Go to God to search you and try you, to examine you and prove your reins. If other helps do not suffice to bring all to an issue, but you are still at a loss, consult some godly and faithful minister or Christian friend. Do not rest till you have put the business of your eternal welfare out of doubt.

'*O Searcher of hearts, set this soul searching, and help him in his search.*'

The miseries of the unconverted

So unspeakably dreadful is the case of every unconverted soul, that I have sometimes thought if I could only convince men that they are still unregenerate, the work were more than half done.

But I find by sad experience that such a spirit of sloth and slumber possesses the unsanctified that, though they are convinced that they are yet unconverted, often they carelessly sit still. Through the love of sensual pleasure, or the hurry of worldly business, or the noise and clamour of earthly cares and lusts and affections, the voice of conscience is drowned, and men go no farther than some cold wishes and general purposes of repenting and amending.

It is therefore of high necessity that I not only convince men that they are unconverted, but that I also endeavour to bring them to a sense of the fearful misery of this state.

But here I find myself aground at first setting off. What tongue can tell the heirs of hell sufficiently of their misery, unless it were Dives in that flame (Lk xvi 24)? Where is the ready writer whose pen can depict their misery who are without God in the world? This cannot fully be done, unless we know the infinite ocean of bliss which is in perfection in God, and from which a state of sin excludes men. '*Who knoweth*', says Moses, '*the power of thine anger?*' (Ps xc 11). And how shall I tell men that which I do not know? Yet so much we know, as one would think would shake the heart of that man that had the least degree of spiritual life and sense.

But this is yet the more perplexing difficulty, that I am to speak to them that are without spiritual sense. Alas! this is not the least part of man's misery, that he is dead, dead in trespasses and sins.

Could I bring paradise into view, or represent the kingdom of heaven to as much advantage as the tempter did the kingdoms of the world, and the glory thereof, to our Saviour; or could I uncover the face of the deep and devouring gulf of Tophet in all its terrors, and open the gates of the infernal furnace; alas, he has no eyes to see it. Could I paint the beauties of holiness or the glory of the Gospel; or could I expose to view the more than diabolical deformity and ugliness of sin; he can no more judge of the loveliness and beauty of the one, and the filthiness and hatefulness of the other, than a blind man of colours. He is alienated from the life of God, through the ignorance that is in him because of the blindness of his heart (Eph iv 18). He neither knows nor can know the things of God, because they are spiritually discerned (1 Cor ii 14). His eyes cannot be savingly opened but by converting grace (Acts xxvi 18). He is a child of darkness, and walks in darkness. Yea, the light in him is darkness.

Shall I ring his knell, or read his sentence, or sound in his ear the terrible trump of God's judgments, that one would think should make both his ears tingle, and strike him into Belshazzar's fit, even to change his countenance, loose his joints, and make his knees smite one against another? Alas, he perceives me not; he has no ears to hear. Or shall I call up the daughters of music, and sing the song of Moses and the Lamb? Yet he will not be stirred. Shall I allure him with the joyful sound, and lovely song, and glad tidings of the Gospel; with the most sweet and inviting calls, comforts, and cordials of the divine promises so exceedingly great and precious? It will not affect him savingly unless I could find him ears as well as tell him the news.

What then shall I do? Shall I show him the lake that burneth with fire and brimstone; or shall I open the box of spikenard, very precious, that fills the whole house of the universe with its perfume, and hope that the savour of Christ's ointments and the

[81]

smell of His garments will attract him? Alas! dead sinners are like the dumb idols; *they have mouths, but they speak not; eyes have they, but they see not; they have ears, but they hear not; noses have they, but they smell not; they have hands, but they handle not; feet have they, but they walk not; neither speak they through their throat.* They are destitute of spiritual sense and motion.

But let me try the sense that last leaves us, and draw the sword of the Word; yet, though I choose mine arrows from God's quiver, and direct them to the heart, nevertheless he does not feel it; for how should he, being past feeling? (Eph iv 19). So that, though '*the wrath of God abideth on him*', and the mountainous weight of so many sins, yet he goes up and down as light as if nothing ailed him. In a word, he carries a dead soul in a living body, and his flesh is but the walking coffin of a corrupt mind that is twice dead (Jude 12).

Which way then shall I come at the miserable object that I have to deal with? Who shall make the heart of stone relent, or the lifeless carcase to feel and move? That God who is able of stones to raise up children unto Abraham, that raises the dead, and melts the mountains, and strikes water out of the flint, that loves to work beyond the hopes and belief of man, that peoples His church with dry bones – He is able to do this. Therefore I bow my knee to the most high God, and as our Saviour prayed at the sepulchre of Lazarus, and the Shunnamite ran to the man of God for her dead child, so your mourning minister carries you in the arms of prayer to that God in whom your help is found.

'*O Thou all-powerful Jehovah, who workest, and none can hinder Thee, who has the keys of death and hell, pity Thou the dead souls that lie here entombed, and roll away the grave-stone, and say as to the dead body of Lazarus, Come forth. Lighten Thou this darkness, O inaccessible Light, and let the day-spring from on high visit the dark regions of the dead, to whom I speak; for Thou canst open the eye that death itself hath closed. Thou that formedst the ear, canst restore the hearing; say Thou to these ears, Ephphatha, and they shall be opened. Give Thou eyes to see Thine excellencies, a taste that may relish Thy sweetness, a scent that may savour Thy ointment, a feeling that may discern the privilege of Thy favour, the burden of Thy wrath, the intolerable weight of unpardoned sin; and give Thy servant order to prophesy to dry bones, and let the effects of this prophecy be as of Thy prophet when he prophesied the valley of dry bones into a living army exceeding great.'*

But I must proceed, as I am able, to unfold that misery which, I confess, no tongue can unfold, no heart can sufficiently comprehend. Know therefore that while you are unconverted:

1: The infinite God is engaged against you. It is no small part of your misery that you are without God. How does Micah run crying after the Danites, '*Ye have taken away my gods, and what have I more?*' (Jgs xviii 24). Oh what a mourning then must you lift up, who are without God, who can lay no claim to Him without daring usurpation! How piercing a moan is that of Saul in his last extremity, '*The Philistines are upon me, and God is departed from me*' (1 Sam xxviii 15). Sinners, what will you do in the day of your visitation? Where will you flee to for help? Where will you leave your glory? What will you do when the Philistines are upon you; when the world shall take its eternal leave of you; when you must bid your friends, houses, and lands, farewell for evermore? What then, I say, will you do, who have not God to go to? Will you call on Him? Will you cry to Him for help? Alas, He will not own you. He will not take any notice of you, but will send you away with '*I never knew you. Depart from me, ye that work iniquity*' (Mt vii 23).

They who know what it is to have a God to go to, a God to live upon – they know a little what a fearful misery it is to be without God. This made a holy man cry out, 'Let me have God or nothing. Let me know Him and His will, and what will please Him, and how I may come to enjoy Him, or would I never had an understanding to know anything!'

But you are not only without God, but God is against you. Oh if God would stand neutral, though He did not own nor help the poor sinner, his case were not so deeply miserable. Though God should give up the poor creature to the will of his enemies, to do their worst with him; though He should deliver him over to the tormentors, that devils should tear and torture him to their utmost power and skill, yet this were not half so fearful. But God will set Himself against the sinner; and, believe it, '*It is a fearful thing to fall into the hands of the living God*' (Heb x 31). There is no friend like Him, no enemy like Him. As much as heaven is above the earth, omnipotence above impotence, so much more terrible is it to fall into the hands of the living God, than into the paws of bears and lions, yea, furies or devils. God Himself will be your tormentor; your destruction shall come from the presence of the Lord (2 Thess i 9).

If God be against you, who shall be for you? '*If one man sin against another, the judge shall judge him: but if a man sin against the Lord, who shall entreat for him?*' (1 Sam ii 25). '*Thou, even thou, art to be feared; and who shall stand in thy sight when thou art angry?*' (Ps lxxvi 7). Who or what shall deliver you out of His hands? Can money? '*Riches profit not in the day of wrath*' (Prov xi 4). Can kings or warriors? No; '*they shall cry to the mountains and rocks to fall on them; and hide them from the face of Him that sitteth on the throne, and from the wrath of the Lamb; for the great day of his wrath is come, and who shall be able to stand?*' (Rev. vi 15-17).

Sinner, I think this should go like a dagger to your heart, to know that God is your enemy. Oh where will you go? Where will you shelter yourself? There is no hope for you, unless you lay down your weapons and sue out your pardon, and get Christ to stand as your friend and make your peace. If it were not for this, you might go into some howling wilderness, and there pine in sorrow, and run mad for anguish of heart and horrible despair. But in Christ there is a possibility of mercy for you, yea, an offer of mercy to you, that you may have God more for you than He is now against you. But if you will not forsake your sins, nor turn thoroughly and purposefully to God by a sound conversion, the wrath of God abides on you, and He proclaims Himself to be against you, as in the prophet: *'Therefore, thus saith the Lord God, Behold I, even I, am against thee!'* (Ezek v 8).

[1] His face is against you. *'The face of the Lord is against them that do evil, to cut off the remembrance of them'* (Ps xxxiv 16). Woe unto them whom God shall set His face against. When He did but look on the host of the Egyptians, how terrible was the consequence! *'I will set my face against that man, and will make him a sign and a proverb, and will cut him off from the midst of my people; and ye shall know that I am the Lord'* (Ezek xiv 8).

[2] His heart is against you. He hates all the workers of iniquity. Man, does not your heart tremble to think of your being an object of God's hatred? *'Though Moses and Samuel stood before me, yet my mind could not be towards this people: cast them out of my sight'* (Jer xv 1). *'My soul loathed them, and their souls also abhorred me'* (Zech xi 8).

[3] All His attributes are against you.

His *justice* is like a flaming sword unsheathed against you. *'If I whet my glittering sword, and my hand take hold on judgment, I will render vengeance to mine adversaries, and will reward them that hate me: I will make mine arrows drunk with blood'* (Deut xxxii 41–42). So exact is justice that it will by no means clear the guilty. God will not discharge you, He will not hold you guiltless, but will require the whole debt in person from you, unless you can make a Scripture claim to Christ and His satisfaction. When the enlightened sinner looks on justice, and sees the balance in which he must be weighed and the sword by which he must be executed, he feels an earthquake in his breast; but Satan keeps this out of sight and persuades the soul, while he can, that the Lord is all made up of mercy, and so lulls it asleep in sin. Divine justice is exact; it must have satisfaction to the utmost farthing. It denounces *'indignation and wrath, tribulation and anguish to every soul that doeth evil'* (Rom ii 8–9). It *'curseth every one that continueth not in all things written in the book of the law to do them*' (Gal iii 10). The justice of God to the unpardoned sinner who has a sense of his guilt, is more terrible than the sight of the creditor to the bankrupt debtor, of the judge and bench to the robber, or of the irons and gibbet to the guilty murderer. When justice sits upon life and death, what dreadful work does it make with the wretched sinner! '*Bind him hand and foot; cast him into outer darkness; there shall be weeping and gnashing of teeth.*' '*Depart from me, ye cursed, into everlasting fire*' (Mt xxii 13; xxv 41). This is the terrible sentence that justice pronounces. Sinner, by this severe justice must you be tried; and as God liveth, this killing sentence must you hear, unless you repent and be converted.

The *holiness* of God is against you. He is not only angry with you – so He may be with His children – but He has a fixed habitual displeasure against you. God's nature is infinitely contrary to sin, and so He cannot delight in a sinner out of Christ.

Oh what a misery is this, to be out of the favour, yea, under the hatred of God; that God, who can as easily lay aside His nature and cease to be God, as not be contrary to you and detest you, except you be changed and renewed. Oh sinner, how dare you think of the bright and radiant sun of purity, or the beauties, the glory of holiness in God? '*The stars are not pure in his sight.*' '*He humbles himself to behold things that are done in heaven*' (Job xxv 5; Ps cxiii 6). Oh those all-searching eyes of His! What do they spy in you; and have you no interest in Christ neither, that He should plead for you? I think He should hear you crying out, astonished, with the Beth-shemites, '*Who is able to stand before this holy Lord God?*'

The *power* of God is mounted like a mighty cannon against you. The glory of God's power is to be displayed in the amazing confusion and destruction of them that obey not the gospel. He will make His power known in them (Rom ix 22) how mightily He can torment them. For this end He raises them up '*that he might make his power known*' (Rom ix 17). O man, are you able to contend with your Maker?

Sinner, the power of God's *anger* is against you, and power and anger together make fearful work. It were better you had all the world in arms against you than to have the power of God against you. There is no escaping His hands, no breaking His prison. *'The thunder of his power, who can understand?'* (Job xxvi 14). Unhappy man that shall understand it by feeling it! *If he will contend with him, he cannot answer him one of a thousand. He is wise in heart and mighty in strength: who hath hardened himself against him, and prospered? which removeth the mountains, and they know it not; which overturneth them in his anger; which shaketh the earth out of her place, and the pillars thereof tremble; which commandeth the sun, and it riseth not; and sealeth up the stars!* . . . *Who will say unto him, What doest thou? If God will not withdraw his anger, the proud helpers do stoop under him'* (Job ix). And are you a fit match for such an antagonist? *'O consider this, ye that forget God, lest he tear you in pieces, and there be none to deliver'* (Ps l 22). Submit to mercy. Let not dust and stubble stand out against the Almighty. Set not briers and thorns against Him in battle, lest He go through them, and consume them together. But lay hold on His strength that you may make peace with Him (Is xxvii 4–5). *'Woe to him that striveth with his Maker!'* (Is xlv 9).

The *wisdom* of God is set to ruin you. He has ordained His arrows, and prepared instruments of death, and made all things ready (Ps vii 11–13). His counsels are against you to contrive your destruction (Jer xviii 11). He laughs in Himself to see how you will be taken and ensnared in the evil day (Ps xxxvii 13). *'The Lord shall laugh at him, for he seeth that his day is coming.'* He sees how you will come down mightily in a moment, how you will wring your hands, and tear your hair, and eat your flesh, and gnash your teeth for anguish and astonishment of heart, when you see you are fallen irremediably into the pit of destruction.

The *truth* of God is sworn against you. If He is faithful and true, you must perish if you go on. Unless He is false to His Word, you must die, except you repent. '*If we believe not, yet he abideth faithful, he cannot deny himself*' (2 Tim ii 13). He is faithful to His threatenings as well as to His promises, and will show His faithfulness in our destruction, if we believe not. God has told you as plain as it can be spoken, that if He wash you not, you have no part in Him; that if you live after the flesh, you shall die; that except you be converted, you shall in no wise enter into the kingdom of heaven (Jn xiii 8; Rom viii 13; Mt xviii 3). Beloved, as the immutable faithfulness of God in His promise and oath affords believers strong consolation, so it is to unbelievers for strong consternation and confusion.

Oh sinner, tell me, what do you think of all the threatenings of God's Word that stand upon record against you? Do you believe they are true or not? If not, you are a wretched infidel. But, if you do believe them, O heart of adamant that you have, that you can walk up and down in quiet, when the truth and faithfulness of God are engaged to destroy you! The whole book of God testifies against you while you remain unconverted. It condemns you in every leaf, and is to you like Ezekiel's roll, written within and without with lamentation, and mourning, and woe. And all this shall surely come upon you except you repent. '*Heaven and earth shall pass away, but one jot or tittle of this word shall never pass away*' (Mt v 18).

Now, put all this together, and tell me if the case of the unconverted is not deplorably miserable. As we read of some persons that had bound themselves by an oath and a curse to kill Paul; so you must know, O sinner, that all the attributes of the infinite God are bound by an oath to punish you. Oh man, what will you do? Where will you flee? If God's omniscience can find you, you shall not escape. If the true and faithful God will regard His oath, perish you must, except you believe and repent. If the Almighty has power to torment you, you must be perfectly miserable in soul and body to all eternity, unless it be prevented by speedy conversion.

2: The whole creation of God is against you. *'The whole creation'*, says Paul, *'groaneth and travaileth in pain'* (Rom viii 22). But what is it that the creation groans under? The fearful abuse it is subject to in serving the lusts of unsanctified men. And what is it that the creation groans for? For freedom and liberty from this abuse; for the *'creature is not willingly made subject to this bondage'* (Rom viii 20–21). If the irrational and inanimate creatures had speech and reason, they would cry out under it, as a bondage insufferable, to be abused by the ungodly, contrary to their natures and the ends that the great Creator made them for. It is a saying of an eminent divine, 'The liquor that the drunkard drinks, if it had reason, like a man, to know how shamefully it is abused, would groan in the barrel against him, it would groan in the cup against him, groan in his throat, in his stomach against him; it would fly in his face, if it could speak. And if God should open the mouths of His creatures, as He did the mouth of Balaam's ass, the proud man's garment on his back would groan against him. There is not a creature, if it had reason to know how it is abused till a man be converted, but would groan against him. The land would groan to bear him, the air would groan to give him breath, their houses would groan to dislodge them, their beds would groan to ease them, their food to nourish them, their clothes to cover them, and the creature would groan to give them any help and comfort, so long as they live in sin against God.'

I think this should be a terror to an unconverted soul, to think he is a burden to the creation. *'Cut it down; why cumbereth it the ground?'* (Lk xiii 7). If inanimate creatures could but speak, your food would say, 'Lord, must I nourish such a wretch as this, and yield forth my strength for him, to dishonour Thee? No, I will choke him rather, if Thou wilt give commission.' The very air would say, 'Lord, must I give this man breath, to set his tongue against heaven, and scorn Thy people, and vent his pride and wrath, and filthy talk, and belch out oaths and blasphemy against Thee? No, if Thou wilt but say the word, he shall be

[89]

breathless for me.' His poor beast would say, 'Lord, must I carry him upon his wicked designs? No, I will break his bones, I will end his days rather, if I may have but leave from Thee.' A wicked man; the earth groans under him, and hell groans for him, till death satisfies both. While the Lord of hosts is against you, be sure the host of the Lord is against you, and all the creatures as it were up in arms till, upon a man's conversion, the controversy being settled between God and him, He makes a covenant of peace with the creature for him (Job v 22–24; Hosea ii 18–20).

3: Satan has his full power over you. You are fast in the paw of that roaring lion who is greedy to devour (1 Pet v 8); *'in the snare of the devil, led captive by him at his will'* (2 Tim ii 26). This is the spirit that worketh in the children of disobedience (Eph ii 2). His drudges they are, and his lusts they do. He is the ruler of the darkness of this world (Eph vi 12), that is, of ignorant sinners who live in darkness. You pity the poor Indians that worship the devil for their god, but little think it is your own case. It is the common misery of all the unsanctified that the devil is their god. Not that they intend to do him homage. They will be ready to defy him, and him that should say so of them; but all this while they serve him, and live under his government. *'His servants ye are to whom ye obey'* (Rom vi 16). O how many then will be found to be the real servants of the devil, who take themselves for no other than the children of God! He can no sooner offer a sinful delight or opportunity for your unlawful advantage than you embrace it. If he suggests a lie, or prompts you to revenge, you readily obey. If he forbids you to read or pray, you hearken to him, and therefore his servants you are. Indeed, he stands behind the curtain, he acts in the dark, and sinners do not see who sets them working, but all the while he leads them. Doubtless the liar does not intend to serve Satan but his own advantage; yet it is he that stands unobserved and puts the thing into his heart. Undoubtedly Judas when he sold his Master for money, and the Chaldeans and Sabeans when they plundered Job, did not intend to do the devil a pleasure, but to satisfy their own covetous thirst; yet it was he that actuated them in their wickedness (Jn xiii 27; Job i 12, 15, 17). Men may be very slaves and common drudges for the devil and not know it: nay, they may please themselves in thoughts of liberty!

Are you yet in ignorance and not turned from darkness unto light? I fear you are under the power of Satan. Do you live in the wilful practice of any known sin? Know that you are of the devil. Do you live in strife, or envy, or malice? Verily he is your father. O dreadful case! However Satan may provide his slaves with various pleasures, yet it is but to draw them into endless perdition. The serpent comes with the fruit in his mouth but, as with Eve, you do not see the deadly sting. He that is now your tempter will one day be your tormentor. O that I could but make you see how bad a master you serve, how merciless a tyrant you gratify; whose pleasure is to set you on to make your perdition and damnation sure, and to heat the furnace hotter and hotter in which you must burn for millions and millions of ages.

4: The guilt of all your sins lies like a mountain upon you. Poor soul, you do not feel it, but this is that which seals your misery. While unconverted, none of your sins are blotted out, they are all upon record against you. Regeneration and remission are never separated; the unsanctified are unjustified and unpardoned. It is a fearful thing to be in debt, but above all, in God's debt; for there is no arrest so formidable as His, no prison so dreary as His. Look upon an enlightened sinner who feels the weight of his own guilt; oh how frightful are His looks, how fearful are his complaints! His comforts are turned into wormwood, and his moisture into drought, and his sleep is departed from his eyes. He is a terror to himself and all that are about him, and is ready to envy the very stones that lie in the street, because they are without sense and do not feel his misery, and he wishes he had been a dog rather than a man because then death had put an end to his misery; whereas now it will be but the beginning of that which will know no ending.

However you may make light of it now, you will one day find the guilt of unpardoned sin to be a heavy burden. This is a millstone that *'whosoever falleth upon it shall be broken; but upon whomsoever it shall fall, it will grind him to powder'* (Mt xxi 44). The guilt of our sins caused the agony and death of the blessed Saviour. And if it did this in the green tree, what will it do in the dry?

Oh think of your case in time. Can you think of that threat without trembling, *'Ye shall die in your sins'*? (Jn viii 24). Oh, better were it for you to die in a jail, in a ditch, in a dungeon, than die in your sins. If death, as it will take away all your comforts, would take away all your sins too, it were some mitigation; but your sins will follow you when your friends leave you, and all worldly enjoyments shake hands with you. Your sins will not die with you as a prisoner's other debts will; but they will go to judgment with you there to be your accusers; and they will go to hell with you there to be your tormentors. O the work that these will make you! O look over your debts in time; how every one of God's commandments is ready to arrest you, and take you by the throat for the innumerable bonds it has upon you. What will you do, then, when they shall all together come in against you? Hold open the eyes of your conscience to consider this, that you may despair of yourself and be driven to Christ, and fly for refuge to lay hold on the hope that is set before you.

5: Your raging lusts miserably enslave you. While unconverted you are a very servant to sin; it reigns over you, and holds you under its dominion, till you are brought within the bonds of God's covenant. There is not such another tyrant as sin. O the vile and fearful work that it engages its servants in!

Would it not pierce your heart to see a company of poor creatures drudging and toiling to carry together faggots and fuel for their own burning? This is the employment of sin's drudges.

Even while they bless themselves in their unrighteous gains, while they sing in their pleasure, they are but treasuring up vengeance for their eternal burning; they are but adding to the pile of Tophet, and flinging in oil to make the flame rage the fiercer. Who would serve such a master, whose work is drudgery, whose wages are death?

What a woeful spectacle was the poor wretch possessed with the legion! Would it not have grieved your heart to see him among the tombs cutting and wounding himself? This is your case; such is your work; every stroke is a thrust at your heart. Conscience indeed is now asleep; but when death and judgment shall bring you to your senses, then will you feel the anguish in every wound. The convinced sinner is an instance of the miserable bondage of sin. Conscience flies upon him, and tells him the end of these things; and yet he is such a slave to his lusts that on he goes, though he sees it will be his perdition. When the temptation comes, lust breaks the cords of all his vows and promises, and carries him headlong to his own destruction.

6: The furnace of eternal vengeance is heated ready for you. Hell and destruction open their mouths upon you; they gape for you; they groan for you (Is v 14), waiting as it were with a greedy eye as you stand on the brink. If the wrath of men be '*as the roaring of a lion*' (Prov xix 12), '*more heavy than the sand*' (Prov xxvii 3), what is the wrath of the infinite God? If the burning furnace heated in Nebuchadnezzar's fiery rage, when he commanded it to be made seven times hotter, was so fierce as to burn up even those that drew near to throw the three children in, how hot is that burning of the Almighty's fury! Surely this is seventy times seven more fierce. What do you think, O man, of being a faggot in hell to all eternity? '*Can thine heart endure, or can thine hands be strong in the days that I shall deal with thee?*' (Ezek xxii 14). Can you abide the everlasting burnings? Can you dwell with consuming fire, when you shall be as glowing iron in hell, and your whole body and soul shall be as perfectly possessed by God's burning vengeance as the sparkling iron with fire, when heated in the fiercest furnace? Some of the choicest servants of God, when under the hidings of His face, and dreading the effects of His displeasure, have bewailed their condition with bitter lamentations. How then will you endure when God shall pour out all His vials, and set Himself against you to torment you, when He shall make your conscience the tunnel by which He will be pouring His burning wrath into your soul for ever, and when he shall fill all your pores as full of torment as they are now full of sin, when immortality shall be your misery, and to die the death of a brute, and be swallowed in the gulf of annihilation, shall be such a felicity as the whole eternity of wishes and an ocean of tears shall never purchase?

Now you can put off the evil day, and laugh and be merry, and forget the terror of the Lord. But how will you hold out, or hold up, when God casts you into a *'bed of torments'* (Rev ii 22): and makes you to *'lie down in sorrow'* (Is l 11); when roarings and blasphemies shall be your only music, and the wine of the wrath of God, which is poured out without mixture into the cup of His indignation, shall be your only drink (Rev xiv 10)? In a word, when the smoke of your torment shall ascend for ever and ever, and you shall have no rest day and night, no rest in your conscience, no ease in your bones; but you shall be an execration and astonishment, and a curse and a reproach, for evermore (Jer xlii 18)?

Oh sinner, stop here, and consider. If you are a man, and not a senseless block, consider. Think where you are standing – upon the very brink of destruction. As the Lord liveth, and as your soul liveth, there is but a step between you and this. You do not know when you lie down, but you may be in hell before morning. You do not know when you rise up, but you may drop in before night. Dare you make light of this? Will you go on in such a dreadful condition, as if nothing ailed you? If you put it off and say that this does not belong to you, look again over the previous chapter, and tell me the truth. Are none of those black

[94]

marks found upon you? Do not blind your eyes. Do not deceive yourself. See your misery while you may prevent it. Think what it is to be a vile outcast, a lost reprobate, a vessel of wrath, into which the Lord will be pouring out His tormenting fury while He has a being. Divine wrath is a fierce, devouring, everlasting, unquenchable fire, and this must be your portion, unless you consider your ways, and speedily turn to the Lord by a sound conversion.

Sinner, it is in vain to flatter you: this would be but to draw you into the unquenchable fire. Know from the living God that here you must lie; with these burnings you must dwell till immortality die and immutability change, till eternity run out and omnipotence is no longer able to punish, except you be in good earnest renewed by sanctifying grace.

7: The law discharges all its threats and curses at you. Oh how dreadfully does it thunder! It flashes devouring fire in your face. Its words are as drawn swords, and as the sharp arrows of the mighty. It demands satisfaction to the utmost, and cries, Justice! Justice! It speaks blood, and war, and wounds, and death, against you. O man away to your stronghold; away from your sins; haste to the sanctuary, the city of refuge – even the Lord Jesus Christ. Hide in Him, or else you are lost, without any hope of recovery.

8: The gospel itself binds the sentence of eternal damnation upon you. If you continue in your impenitent and unconverted state, know that the Gospel denounces a much sorer condemnation than ever would have been for the transgression only of the first covenant. Is it not a dreadful case to have the Gospel itself fill its mouth with threats; to have the Lord to roar from Mount Zion against you? (Joel iii 16). Hear the terror of the Lord. '*He that believeth not shall be damned.*' '*Except ye repent, ye shall all perish.*' '*This is the condemnation, that light is come into the world, and men loved darkness rather than light.*' '*He that believeth* *not, the wrath of God abideth on him.' 'If the word spoken by angels was steadfast, and every transgression and disobedience received a just recompense of reward, how shall we escape if we neglect so great salvation?' 'He that despised Moses' law died without mercy: of how much sorer punishment shall he be thought worthy who hath trodden under foot the Son of God?'* (Mk xvi 16; Lk xiii 3; Jn iii 19, 36; Heb ii 2, 3; Heb x 28–29).

And is this true indeed? Is this your misery? Yea, it is as true as God is. Better open your eyes and see it now while you may remedy it, than blind and harden yourself till, to your eternal sorrow, you shall feel what you would not believe. And if it is true, what do you mean by lingering and loitering in such a state as this?

Alas for you, poor man! How effectually has sin undone you, depraved you and despoiled you even of your reason to look after your own everlasting good! O miserable wretch! What stupidity and senselessness have surprised you! Oh let me knock and awake this sleeper! Who dwells within the walls of this flesh? Is there a soul here, a rational, understanding soul; or are you only a senseless lump?

Are you a rational soul, and yet so far brutified as to forget that you are immortal, and to think yourself to be as the beasts that perish? Having reason to understand the eternity of the future state, do you yet make light of being everlastingly miserable, which is to be so much below the brute, as it is worse to act against reason than to act without it? Oh unhappy soul, that was the glory of man, the companion of angels, and the image of God; that was God's representative in the world, and had the supremacy amongst the creatures, and the dominion over your Maker's works; are you now become a slave to sense? Are you heaping together a little refined earth, so unsuited to your spiritual immortal nature? Oh why do you not consider where you will spend eternity? Death is at hand; the Judge is even at the door. Yet a little while, and *'time shall be no longer'*. And will you run the hazard of continuing in such a state, in which, if you are overtaken, you are irrecoverably miserable?

Come then, arise, and attend to your nearest concerns. Tell me where you are going? What! will you live in such a course, in which every act is a step to perdition; and you do not know but the next night you may make your bed in hell? Oh, if you have a spark of reason, consider, and turn and hearken to your true friend, who would show you your present misery, that you might in time make your escape, and be eternally happy.

Hear what the Lord saith. '*Fear ye not me? saith the Lord: will ye not tremble at my presence?*' (Jer v 22). O sinners, do you make light of the wrath to come? I am sure there is a time coming when you will not make light of it. Why! the very devils believe and tremble. What! are you more hardened than they? Will you run upon the edge of the precipice? Will you play at the hole of the asp? Will you put your hand into the cockatrice's den? Will you dally with devouring wrath as if you were indifferent whether you escape or endure it? There is no one so beside himself as the wilful sinner, that goes on in his unconverted state without sense, as if nothing ailed him. The man that runs into the cannon's mouth and sports with his blood, or lets out his life in a frolic, is sensible, sober, and serious, compared with him that goes on still in his trespasses. '*For he stretcheth out his hand against God, and strengtheneth himself against the Almighty: he runneth upon him, even upon his neck, upon the thick bosses of his bucklers*' (Job xv 25–26). Is it wisdom to sport with the second death, or to venture into the lake that burneth with fire and brimstone? What shall I say? I can find no expression, no comparison, by which to set forth the dreadful madness of the soul that will go on in sin.

Awake! awake! O sinner, arise and take your flight. There is but one door that you may flee by, and that is the narrow door of conversion and the new birth. Unless you turn unfeignedly from all your sins, and come to Jesus Christ, and take Him for the Lord your righteousness, and walk in Him in holiness and newness of life; as the Lord liveth, it is not more certain that you are now out of hell, than that you shall without fail be in it but a few days or nights from now. Oh set your heart to think of your case. Does not your everlasting misery or welfare deserve a little consideration? Look again over the miseries of the unconverted. If the Lord has not spoken by me, regard me not; but if it is the very word of God that all this misery lies upon you, what a state you are in! Is it for one that has his senses to live in such a condition, and not to make all possible haste to prevent his utter ruin? O man, who has bewitched you that in the matters of this present life you shall be wise enough to forecast your business, foresee your danger, and prevent your ruin; but in matters of everlasting consequence shall be slight and careless, as if they little concerned you? Is it nothing to you to have all the attributes of God engaged against you? Can you live without His favour? Can you escape His hands, or endure His vengeance? Do you hear the creation groaning under you, and hell groaning for you, and yet think your case good enough? Are you under the power of corruption, in the dark, noisome prison, fettered with lusts, working out your own damnation – and is this not worth a thought? Will you make light of all the terrors of the law, of all its curses and thunders, as if they were but the threatenings of a child? Do you laugh at hell and destruction, or can you drink the envenomed cup of the Almighty's fury, as if it were but a common potion?

Gird up now your loins like a man, for I will demand of thee, and answer thou me. Are you such a leviathan as that the scales of your pride should resist your Maker? Will you esteem His arrows as straw, and the instruments of death as rotten wood? Are you chief of all the children of pride, even that you should count His darts as stubble, and laugh at the shaking of His spear? Do you mock at fear, and are you not frightened, do you not turn back from God's sword when His quiver rattles against you, the glittering spear and the shield? Well, if the threats and calls of the Word will not awaken you, I am sure death and judgment will. Oh what will you do when the Lord comes forth against you, and in His fury falls upon you, and you shall feel what you now read?

If when Daniel's enemies were cast into the den of lions, both they and their wives and their children, the lions had the mastery over them and broke all their bones in pieces ere they came to the bottom of the den, what shall become of you when you fall into the hands of the living God?

Oh, do not then contend with God. Repent and be converted, so none of this shall come upon you. '*Seek ye the Lord while he may be found; call ye upon him while he is near. Let the wicked forsake his way, and the unrighteous man his thoughts: and let him return unto the Lord, and he will have mercy upon him, and to our God, for he will abundantly pardon*' (Is lv 6–7).

6

Directions to the unconverted

Before you read these directions, I advise you, yea, I charge you before God and His holy angels, that you resolve to follow them, as far as conscience shall be convinced of their agreeableness to God's Word and your state; and call in His assistance and blessing that they may succeed. And as I have sought the Lord and consulted His oracles as to what advice to give you, so must you entertain it with that awe, reverence, and purpose of obedience, which the word of the living God requires.

Now, then, attend. '*Set your heart unto all that I shall testify unto you this day; for it is not a vain thing – it is your life*' (Deut xxxii 46). This is the aim of all that has been spoken hitherto, to bring you to set your heart upon turning to God. I would not trouble you, nor torment you before the time with the thoughts of your eternal misery, but in order that you may make your escape. Were you shut up under your present misery without remedy, it were but mercy to let you alone, that you might take in that little poor comfort which you are capable of in this world; but you may yet be happy, if you do not wilfully refuse the means of your recovery. Behold, I hold open the door to you; arise, take your flight. I set the way of life before you; walk in it, and you shall live, and not die. It grieves me that you should be your own murderers, and throw yourselves headlong, when God and man cry out to you, as Peter in another case to his Master, 'Spare thyself.'

The destruction of ungodly men is wilful. God that made them cries out to them, as Paul to the jailer when about to murder himself, '*Do thyself no harm*.' The ministers of Christ forewarn them, and follow them, and would gladly have them back; but alas! no expostulations or entreaties will prevail, but men will hurl themselves into perdition, while pity itself looks on.

What shall I say? Would it not grieve a person of any humanity, if, in the time of a raging plague, he should have a remedy that would infallibly cure all the country and recover the most hopeless patients, and yet his friends and neighbours should die by hundreds around him, because they would not use it? Men and brethren, though you carry the certain symptoms of death on your faces, yet I have a prescription that will cure you all infallibly. Follow these directions, and if you do not then win heaven, I will be content to lose it.

Hear, then, O sinner, and as ever you would be converted and saved, take the following counsel.

1: Set it down with yourself as an undoubted truth, that it is impossible for you ever to get to heaven in this your unconverted state.

Can any other but Christ save you? and He tells you He will never do it except you be regenerated and converted. Does He not keep the keys of heaven, and can you go in without His leave? as you must, if ever you go in your natural condition, without a sound and thorough conversion.

2: Labour to get a thorough sight and lively sense and feeling of your sins.

Till men are weary and heavy laden, and pricked at the heart, and quite sick of sin, they will not come to Christ for cure, nor sincerely enquire, '*What shall we do?*' They must see themselves as dead men, before they will come unto Christ that they may live. Labour, therefore, to set all your sins in order before you; do not be afraid to look upon them, but let your spirit make diligent search. Enquire into your heart, and into your life; enter into a thorough examination of yourself and all your ways, that you may make a full discovery; and call in the help of God's Spirit, out of a sense of your own inability to do this by yourself, for it is His proper work to convince of sin. Spread all before your conscience, till your heart and eyes are set weeping. Do not leave striving with God and your own soul, till it cry out under the sense of your sins, as the enlightened jailer, '*What must I do to be saved?*' To this purpose,

Meditate on the number of your sins. David's heart failed when he thought of this, and considered that he had more sins than the hairs of his head. This made him cry out for the multitude of God's tender mercies. The loathsome carcase does not more hatefully swarm with crawling maggots, than an unsanctified soul with filthy lusts. They fill the head, the heart, the eyes and mouth of him. Look backward; where was ever the place, what was ever the time, in which you did not sin? Look inward; what part or power can you find in soul or body which is not poisoned with sin; what duty do you ever perform, into which this poison is not shed? Oh how great is the sum of your debts, who have been all your life running upon trust, and never did or can pay off one penny! Look over the sin of your nature, and all its cursed brood, the sins of your life. Call to mind your omissions and commissions; the sins of your thoughts, words, and actions; the sins of your youth, and the sins of your riper years. Do not be like a desperate bankrupt that is afraid to look over his books. Read the records of conscience carefully. These books must be opened sooner or later.

Meditate upon the aggravations of your sins, as they are the grand enemies of the God of your life, and of the life of your soul; in a word, they are the public enemies of all mankind. How do David, Ezra, Daniel, and the good Levites, aggravate their sins, from the consideration of their opposition to God and His good and righteous laws, and of the mercies and warnings against which they were committed! Oh the work that sin has done in the world! This is the enemy that has brought in death; that has robbed and enslaved man, that has turned the world upside down, and sown the dissensions between man and the creatures, between man and man, yea, between man and himself, setting the animal part against the rational, the will against the judgment, lust against conscience; yea, worst of all, between God and man, making the sinner both hateful to God and the hater of God. O man, how can you make so light of sin? This is the traitor that thirsted for the blood of the Son of God, that sold Him, that mocked Him, that scourged Him, that spat in His face, that tore His hands, that pierced His side, that pressed His soul, that mangled His body, that never left Him till he had bound Him, condemned Him, nailed Him, crucified Him, and put Him to an open shame. This is that deadly poison, so powerful of operation that one drop of it, shed on the root of mankind, has corrupted, spoiled, poisoned, and ruined the whole race. This is the bloody executioner that has killed the prophets, burned the martyrs, murdered all the apostles, all the patriarchs, all the kings and potentates; that has destroyed cities, swallowed empires, and devoured whole nations. Whatever weapon it was done by, it was sin that caused the execution. Do you yet think it only a small thing? If Adam and all his children could be dug out of their graves, and their bodies piled up to heaven, and an inquest were made as to what matchless murderer were guilty of all this blood, it would be all found in sin. Study the nature of sin, till your heart incline to fear and loathe it; and meditate on the aggravations of your particular sins, how you have sinned against all God's warnings, against your own prayers, against mercies, against corrections, against clearest light, against freest love, against your own resolutions, against promises, vows, and covenants of better obedience. Charge your heart with these things till it blush for shame, and be brought out of all good opinion of itself.

Meditate on the desert of sin. It cries to Heaven; it calls for vengeance. Its due wages are death and damnation; it brings the curse of God upon the soul and body. The least sinful word or thought lays you under the infinite wrath of God. O what a load of wrath, what a weight of curses, what treasures of vengeance, have all the millions of your sins deserved! Oh judge yourself that the Lord may not judge you.

Meditate on the deformity and defilement of sin. It is black as hell, the very image and likeness of the devil drawn upon the soul. It would terrify you to see yourself in the hateful deformity of your nature. There is no mire so unclean, no plague or leprosy so noisome as sin, in which you are plunged and rendered more displeasing to the pure and holy nature of the glorious God than the vilest object can be to you. Could you take up a toad into your bosom; could you cherish it, and take delight in it? But you are as contrary to the pure and perfect holiness of the divine nature, till you are purified by the blood of Jesus and the power of renewing grace.

Above all other sins, consider these two.

[1] The sin of your heart. It is to little purpose to lop off the branches while the root of corruption remains untouched. In vain do men lave out the streams, when the fountain is running that fills up all again. Let the axe of your repentance, with David's go to the root of sin. Study how deep, how permanent is your natural pollution, how universal it is, till you cry out, with Paul, against your body of death. The heart is never soundly broken till thoroughly convinced of the heinousness of its original and deep-rooted depravity. Here fix your thoughts; this is that which makes you backward to all good, and prone to all evil; that sheds blindness, pride, prejudice, and unbelief into your mind; enmity, inconstancy, and obstinacy into your will; inordinate heats and colds into your affections; insensibleness and unfaithfulness into your conscience; slipperiness into your memory. In a word, it has put every wheel of the soul out of order, and made it, from a habitation of holiness, to become a very hell of iniquity. This is what has defiled and perverted all your members, and turned them into weapons of unrighteousness, and servants of sin; that has filled the head with carnal and corrupt designs, the hand with sinful practices, the eyes with wandering and wantonness, the

tongue with deadly poison. This is what has opened the ears to tales, flattery and filthy talk, and shut them against the instructions of life; and has rendered your heart the cursed source of all deadly imaginations, so that it pours out its wickedness without ceasing even as naturally as a fountain pours forth its waters, or the raging sea casts forth mire and dirt. And will you yet be in love with yourself, and tell us any longer of your good heart? Oh never leave meditating on the desperate contagion, the original corruption of your heart, till, with Ephraim, you bemoan yourself; and with the deepest shame and sorrow smite on your breast, as the publican; and, with Job, abhor yourself and repent in dust and ashes.

[2] The particular evil that you are most addicted to. Find out all its aggravations; set home upon your heart all God's threats against it. Repentance drives before it the whole herd, but especially sticks the arrow in the beloved sin, and singles this out, above the rest, to run it down. Oh labour to make this sin odious to your soul, and double your guard and resolutions against it, because this is most dishonouring to God and dangerous to you.

3: Strive to affect your heart with a deep sense of your present misery.

Read over the previous chapter again and again, and get it out of the book into your heart. Remember when you lie down, that for all you know, you may awake in flames; and when you rise up, that by the next night you may make your bed in hell. Is it nothing to you to live in such a fearful state, to stand tottering on the brink of the bottomless pit; and to live at the mercy of every disease that, if it but fall upon you, will send you forthwith into the burnings? Suppose you saw a condemned wretch hanging over Nebuchadnezzar's burning fiery furnace by nothing but a thread which was ready to break every moment, would not your heart tremble for such a one? Thou art the man: this is your very case, O man, woman, who reads this, if you are yet unconverted. What if the thread of your life should break – and you know not but it may be the next night, yea, the next moment – where would you be then? Where would you drop? Verily, upon the breaking of this thread, you fall into the lake that burns with fire and brimstone, where you must lie while God has a being, if you die in your present state. And does not your soul tremble as you read? Do not your tears wet the paper, and your heart throb in your bosom? Do you not yet begin to smite on your breast, and think with yourself what need you have of a change? Oh what is your heart made of? Have you not only lost all regard to God, but all love and pity to yourself?

O study your misery till your heart cry out for Christ as earnestly as ever a drowning man did for a boat, or the wounded for a surgeon. Men must come to see the danger and feel the smart of their deadly sores and sickness, or Christ will be to them a physician of no value. The manslayer hastens to the city of refuge, when pursued by the avenger of blood; but men must be even forced and driven out of themselves, or they will not come to Christ. It was distress and extremity that made the prodigal think of returning. While Laodicea thinks herself rich, increased in goods, in need of nothing, there is little hope. She must be deeply convinced of her wretchedness, blindness, poverty, and nakedness, before she will come to Christ for His gold, raiment, and eye-salve. Therefore hold the eyes of conscience open, amplify your misery as much as possible, do not flee the sight of it for fear it should fill you with terror. The sense of your misery is but as it were the festering of the wound, which is necessary to the cure. Better now to fear the torments that await you, than to feel them hereafter.

4: Settle it in your heart that you must look out of yourself and away from your own doings for help.

Do not think your praying, reading, hearing, confessing, or amending, will effect the cure. These must be attended to, but you are undone if you rest in them. You are a lost man if you hope to escape drowning on any other plank but Jesus Christ.

You must unlearn yourself, and renounce your own wisdom, your own righteousness, your own strength, and throw yourself wholly upon Christ, or you cannot escape. While men trust in themselves, and establish their own righteousness, and have confidence in the flesh, they will not come savingly to Christ. You must know your gain to be but loss, your strength but weakness, your righteousness rags and rottenness, before there will be an effectual closure between Christ and you. Can the lifeless body shake off its grave-clothes, and loose the bands of death? Then may you recover yourself, who are dead in trespasses and sins, and under an impossibility of serving your Maker acceptably in this condition. Therefore, when you go to pray or meditate, or to do any of the duties to which you are here directed, go out of yourself, and call in the help of the Spirit, as despairing to do anything pleasing to God in your own strength. Yet do not neglect duty. While the eunuch was reading, then the Holy Ghost did send Philip to him. When the disciples were praying, when Cornelius and his friends were hearing, then the Holy Ghost fell upon and filled them all.

5: Henceforth renounce all your sins.

If you yield yourself to the practice of any sin, you are undone. In vain do you hope for life by Christ, except you depart from iniquity. Forsake your sins, or you cannot find mercy. You cannot be married to Christ except you be divorced from sin. Give up the traitor, or you can have no peace with heaven. Keep not Delilah in your lap. You must part with your sins or with your soul: spare but one sin and God will not spare you. Your sins must die, or you must die for them. If you allow one sin, though but a little, a secret one, though you may plead necessity, and have a hundred shifts and excuses for it, the life of your soul must go for the life of that sin. And will it not be dearly bought?

O sinner, hear and consider. If you will part with your sins, God will give you His Christ. Is not this a fair exchange? I testify unto you this day, that if you perish, it is not because there was never a Saviour provided nor life tendered, but because, with

the Jews, you prefer the murderer before the Saviour, sin before
Christ, and love darkness rather than light. Search your heart
therefore with candles, as the Jews did their houses for leaven
before the passover. Labour to find out your sins; enter into your
closet, and consider . . . What evil have I lived in? . . . What duty
have I neglected towards God? . . . what sin have I lived in against
my brother? And now strike the darts through the heart of your
sin, as Joab did through Absalom's. Do not stand looking at your
sins, nor rolling the morsel under your tongue, but cast it out as
poison, with fear and detestation. Alas, what will your sins do for
you that you should hesitate to part with them? They will flatter
you, but they will undo you and poison you while they please you,
and arm the justice and wrath of the infinite God against you.
They will open hell for you, and pile up fuel to burn you. Behold
the gibbet that they have prepared for you. O treat them like
Haman, and do upon them the execution they would else have
done upon you. Away with them, crucify them and let Christ only
be Lord over you.

6: Make a solemn choice of God for your portion and blessedness.

With all possible devotion and veneration avouch the Lord
for your God. Set the world, with all its glory, and paint, and
gallantry, with all its pleasures and promotions, on the one hand;
and set God, with all His infinite excellencies and perfections, on
the other; and see that you do deliberately make your choice.
Take up your rest in God. Sit down under His shadow. Let His
promises and perfections turn the scale against all the world.
Settle it in your heart, that the Lord is an all-sufficient portion,
that you cannot be miserable while you have God to live upon.
Take Him for your shield and exceeding great reward. God alone
is more than all the world; content yourself with Him. Let
others possess the preferments and glory of the world; but do you
place your happiness in the favour of God, and in the light of His
countenance.

Poor sinner, you have fallen off from God, and have engaged

His power and wrath against you; yet know, that of His abundant grace He offers to be your God again in Christ. What do you say? Will you have the Lord for your God? Take this counsel, and you shall have Him. Come to Him by Christ, renounce the idols of your pleasures, gain, reputation. Let these be pulled from their throne, and set God's interest uppermost in your heart. Take Him as God, to be chief in your affections and purposes; for He will not endure to have any set above Him. In a word, you must take Him in all His personal relations and in all His essential perfections.

[1] In all His personal relations. God the Father must be taken for your Father. O come to Him with the prodigal: *'Father, I have sinned against heaven, and in thy sight, and am not worthy to be called thy son;* but since of Thy wonderful mercy Thou art pleased to take me, that am of myself most vile, even a beast and no man before Thee, to be a child, I solemnly take Thee for my Father, commend myself to Thy care, and trust to Thy providence, and cast my burden on Thee. I depend on Thy provision, and submit to Thy corrections, and trust under the shadow of Thy wings, and hide in Thy chambers, and fly to Thy name. I renounce all confidence in myself; I repose my confidence in Thee. I declare my engagement with Thee; I will be for Thee, and not for another.'

God the Son must be taken for your Saviour, your Redeemer, and your Righteousness. He must be accepted, as the only way to the Father, and the only means of life. O then put off the raiment of your captivity, put on the wedding garment, and go and marry yourself to Christ. 'Lord, I am Thine, and all I have, my body, soul, and estate. I give my heart to Thee; I will be Thine undividedly, Thine everlastingly. I will set Thy name on all I have, and use it only as Thy goods, during Thy absence, resigning all to Thee. I will have no king but Thee to reign over me. Other lords have had dominion over me; but now I will make mention of Thy name only, and do here take an oath of fidelity to Thee, promising to serve and fear Thee above all competitors. I reject my own righteousness, and despair of ever being pardoned and saved for my own duties or graces, and lean solely on Thy all-sufficient sacrifice and intercession for pardon, life, and acceptance before God. I take Thee for my only Guide and Instructor, resolving to be directed by Thee, and to wait for Thy counsel.'

Lastly, God the Spirit must be taken for your Sanctifier, for your Advocate, your Counsellor, your Comforter, the Teacher of your ignorance, the Pledge and Earnest of your inheritance. '*Awake, thou North wind, and come, thou South, and blow upon my garden*' (Cant iv 16). 'Come, Thou Spirit of the Most High; here is a temple for Thee; do Thou rest here for ever; dwell here. Lo, I give possession to Thee, full possession; I send Thee the keys of my heart, that all may be Thine. I give up the use of all to Thee, that every faculty and every member may be Thy instrument to work righteousness and do the will of my Father who is in heaven.'

[2] In all His essential perfections. Consider how the Lord has revealed Himself to you in His Word. Will you take Him as such a God? O sinner, here is the most blessed news that ever came to the sons of men: The Lord will be your God, if you will but close with Him in His excellencies. Will you have the merciful, the gracious, the sin-pardoning God to be your God? 'O yes,' says the sinner, 'otherwise I am undone.' But He further tells you, 'I am the holy and sin-hating God; if you will be owned as one of My people, you must be holy – holy in heart, holy in life. You must put away all your iniquities, be they ever so dear, ever so natural, ever so necessary to the maintaining of your worldly interest. Unless you will be at enmity with sin, I cannot be your God. Cast out the leaven. Put away the evil of thy doings; cease to do evil; learn to do well. Bring forth Mine enemies, or there is no peace to be had with Me.' What does your heart answer? 'Lord, I desire to be holy as Thou art holy, and to be made partaker of Thy holiness. I love Thee, not only for Thy goodness and mercy, but for Thy holiness and purity. I take Thy holiness for my happiness. O be to me a fountain of holiness. Set on me

the stamp and impress of Thy holiness. I will thankfully part with all my sins at Thy command. My wilful sins I do henceforth forsake; and for mine infirmities that cleave unto me, though I would be rid of them, I will strive against them continually. I detest them, and will pray against them, and never let them have rest in my soul.' Beloved, whoever of you will thus accept the Lord, He shall be your God.

Again, He tells you, 'I am the all-sufficient God. Will you lay all at My feet, give up all to My disposal, and take Me for your only portion? Will you own and honour my all-sufficiency? Will you take Me as your happiness and treasure, your hope and bliss? I am a sun and a shield all in one; will you have Me for your all?' Now what do you say to this? Does your soul long for the onions and flesh-pots of Egypt? Are you loath to change your earthly happiness for a portion in God; and though you would be glad to have God and the world too, yet can you not think of having Him, and nothing but Him; but had rather take up with the earth below, if God would but let you keep it as long as you would? This is a fearful sign. But now, if you are willing to sell all for the Pearl of great price; if your heart answer, 'Lord, I desire no other portion but Thee. Take the corn and the wine and the oil who will, so I may have the light of Thy countenance. I fix upon Thee for my happiness; I gladly venture myself on Thee, and trust myself with Thee. I set my hope in Thee; I take up my rest with Thee. Let me hear Thee say, "I am thy God, thy salvation," and I have enough, all I wish for. I will make no terms with Thee but for Thyself. Let me have Thee for sure, let me be able to make my claim and see my title to Thyself; and for other things, I leave them to Thee. Give me more or less, anything or nothing; I will be satisfied in my God.' Take Him thus, and He is your own.

Again, He tells you, 'I am the sovereign Lord; if you will have Me for your God you must give Me the supremacy. You must not make Me second to sin or any worldly interest. If you will be My people I must have the rule over you; you must not live at your pleasure. Will you come under My yoke? Will you bow to My government? Will you submit to My discipline, to My Word, to My rod?' Sinner, what do you say to this? 'Lord, I had rather be at Thy command than live at my own will. I had rather have Thy will to be done than mine. I approve of and consent to Thy laws, and account it my privilege to be under them. And though the flesh rebel, and often break its bounds, I have resolved to take no other Lord but Thee. I willingly take the oath of Thy supremacy, and acknowledge Thee for my Sovereign, and resolve all my days to pay the tribute of worship, obedience, love, and service to Thee, and to live to Thee to the end of my life.' This is a right acceptance of God.

To be short, He tells you, 'I am the true and faithful God. If you will have Me for your God you must be content to trust Me. Will you venture yourselves upon My Word, and depend on My faithfulness, and take My bond for your security? Will you be content to follow Me in poverty, and reproach, and affliction here; and to tarry till the next world for your preferment? Will you be content to labour and suffer, and to tarry for your returns till the resurrection of the just? My promise will not always be instantly fulfilled; will you have the patience to wait?' Now, beloved, what do you say to this? Will you have this God for your God? Will you be content to live by faith, and trust Him for an unseen happiness, an unseen heaven, an unseen glory? Do your hearts answer, 'Lord, we will venture ourselves upon Thee. We commit ourselves to Thee, we cast ourselves upon Thee. We know whom we have trusted. We are willing to take Thy word; we prefer Thy promises before our own possessions, and the hopes of heaven before all the enjoyments of earth. We will do Thy pleasure – what Thou wilt here, so that we may have but Thy faithful promise for heaven hereafter.' If you can in trust, and upon deliberation, thus accept of God, He will be yours. Thus there must be, in a right conversion to God, a closing with Him suitable to His excellencies. But when men close with His mercy, but yet love sin, hating holiness and purity; or will take

Him for their Benefactor, but not for their Sovereign; or for their Patron, and not for their Portion; this is no thorough and sound conversion.

7: Accept the Lord Jesus in all His offices as yours. Upon these terms Christ may be had. Sinner, you have undone yourself, and are plunged into the ditch of most deplorable misery, out of which you are never able to escape; but Jesus Christ is able and ready to help you, and He freely tenders Himself to you. Be your sins ever so many, ever so great, or of ever so long continuance, yet you shall be most certainly pardoned and saved, if you do not wretchedly neglect the offer that in the name of God is here made to you. The Lord Jesus calls you to look to Him and be saved. Come unto Him, and He will in no wise cast you out. Yea, He beseeches you to be reconciled. He cries in the streets; He knocks at your door. He invites you to accept Him, and live with Him. If you die, it is because you would not come to Him for life (Is xlv 22; Jn vi 37; 2 Cor v 20; Prov i 20; Rev iii 20; Jn v 40).

Accept an offered Christ now, and you are made for ever. Give your consent to Him now, and the match is made; all the world cannot hinder it. Do not stand off because of your unworthiness. I tell you, nothing can undo you but your own unwillingness. Speak, man; will you give your consent? Will you have Christ in all His relations to be yours, your King, your Priest, your Prophet? Will you have Him and bear His cross? Do not take Christ without consideration, but sit down first and count the cost. Will you lay all at His feet? Will you be content to run all hazards with Him? Will you take your lot with Him, fall where it will? Will you deny yourself, take up your cross, and follow Him? Are you deliberately, understandingly, freely determined to cleave to Him in all times and conditions? If so, you shall never perish, but you have passed from death unto life. Here lies the main point of your salvation, that you be found in your covenant-closure with Jesus Christ; and therefore, if you love yourself, see that you be faithful to God and your soul here.

8: Resign all your powers and faculties, and your whole interest to be His. '*They gave their own selves unto the Lord*' (2 Cor viii 5). '*Present your bodies a living sacrifice*' (Rom xii 1). The Lord seeks not yours, but you. Resign therefore your body with its members to Him, and your soul with all its powers, that He may be glorified in your body and in your spirit, which are His.

In a right closing with Christ all your faculties are given up to Him. Your judgment says, 'Lord, Thou art worthy of all acceptation, Chief of ten thousand: happy is the man that findeth Thee. All the things that are to be desired are not to be compared with Thee' (Prov iii 13–15). The understanding lays aside its corrupt reasonings and cavils, and its prejudices against Christ and His ways. It is now past questioning, and determines for Christ against all the world. It concludes it is good to be here, and sees such a treasure in this field, such a value in this pearl, as is worth all (Mt xiii 44–46). 'O here is the richest prize that ever man was offered; here is the most sovereign remedy that ever mercy prepared. He is worthy of my esteem, worthy of my choice, worthy of my love, worthy to be embraced, adored, admired, for evermore (Rev v 12). I approve of His articles: His terms are righteous and reasonable, full of equity and mercy.' Again, the will resigns. It stands no longer wavering, but is peremptorily determined: 'Lord, Thy love hath overcome me, Thou hast won me, and Thou shalt have me. Come in, Lord; to Thee I freely open; I consent to be saved in Thine own way. Thou shalt have anything – nay, have all, let me have but Thee.' The memory gives up to Christ: 'Lord, here is a storehouse for Thee: out with this trash: lay in the treasures. Let me be a repository of Thy truth, Thy promises, Thy providences.' The conscience comes in: 'Lord, I will ever side with Thee: I will be Thy faithful registrar. I will warn when the sinner is tempted, and smite when Thou art offended. I will witness for Thee, and judge for Thee, and guide into Thy ways, and will never let sin have quiet in this soul.' The affections also come to Christ: 'O,' says Love, 'I am sick for Thee.' 'O,' says Desire, 'now I have what

I sought for. Here is the Desire of nations; here is bread for me, and balm for me: all that I want.' Fear bows the knee with awe and veneration: 'Welcome, Lord, to Thee will I pay my homage. Thy Word and rod shall command my actions; Thee will I reverence and adore; before Thee will I fall down and worship.' Grief likewise puts in: 'Lord, Thy displeasure and Thy dishonour, Thy people's calamities and my own iniquities, shall be what shall set me a-weeping. I will mourn when Thou art offended; I will weep when Thy cause is wounded.' Anger likewise comes in for Christ: 'Lord, nothing so enrages me as my folly against Thee, that I should be so besotted as to hearken to the flatteries of sin and the temptations of Satan against Thee.' Hatred, too, will side with Christ: 'I protest mortal enmity to Thine enemies, that I will never be a friend to Thy foes. I vow an eternal quarrel with every sin. I will give no quarter, I will make no peace.' Thus let all your powers yield to Jesus Christ.

Again, you must give up your whole interest to Him. If there is anything that you keep back from Christ, it will be your undoing (Lk xiv 33). Unless you will forsake all, in preparation and resolution of your heart, you cannot be His disciple. You must hate father and mother, yea, and your own life also, in comparison with Him, and as far as it stands in competition with Him. In a word, you must give Him yourself, and all that you have without reservation, or else you can have no part in Him.

9: Choose the laws of Christ as the rule of your words, thoughts and actions.

This is the true convert's choice. But here remember these three rules. 1. You must choose them all, there is no getting to heaven by a partial obedience. It is not enough to take up the cheap and easy part of religion, and let alone the duties that are costly and self-denying, and oppose the interests of the flesh; you must take all or none. A sincere convert, though he makes conscience of the greatest sins and weightiest duties, yet he makes true conscience of little sins and of all duties. 2. You must choose Christ's laws for all times, for prosperity and adversity. A true convert is resolved in his course; he will stand to his choice, and will not set his back to the wind, and be of the religion of the times. '*I have stuck to thy testimonies; I have inclined my heart to perform thy statutes always, even to the end. Thy testimonies have I taken as a heritage for ever. I will have respect to thy statutes continually*' (Ps cxix). 3. This must be done deliberately and understandingly. The disobedient son said, 'I go, sir,' but he went not. How fairly did they promise, '*All that the Lord our God shall speak unto thee we will do it!*' And it is likely they meant what they said. But when it came to the trial it was found that there was not such a heart in them as to do what they had promised (Deut v 27, 29).

If you would be sincere in closing with the laws and the ways of Christ, study the meaning, and breadth, and extent of them. Remember that they are spiritual; they reach the very thoughts and inclinations of the heart; so that, if you will walk by this rule, your very thoughts and inward motions must be under government. Again, they are very strict and self-denying, quite contrary to your natural inclinations. You must take the strait gate, the narrow way, and be content to have the flesh curbed from the liberty it desires. In a word, they are very large, for '*thy commandment is exceeding broad*' (Ps cxix 96).

Do not rest in general commands, for there is much deceit in them, but bring down your heart to the particular commands of Christ. Those Jews, in the prophet, seemed as well resolved as any in the world, and called God to witness that they meant as they said. But they rested in generals. When God's command crosses their inclination, they will not obey (Jer xlii 1–6, xliii 2). Take the Westminster Assembly's Larger Catechism, and see their excellent and most comprehensive exposition of the commandments, and put your heart to it. Are you resolved, in the strength of Christ, to set upon the conscientious practice of every duty that you find to be required of you, and to set against every sin that you find to be forbidden? This is the way to be sound in God's statutes, that you may never be ashamed (Ps cxix 80).

Observe the special duties that your heart is most against, and the special sins that it is most inclined to, and see whether it be truly resolved to perform the one and forgo the other. What do you say to your bosom sin, your profitable sin? What do you say to costly, hazardous, and flesh-displeasing duties? If you halt here, and do not resolve, by the grace of God, to cross the flesh and be in earnest, you are unsound.

10: Let all this be completed in a solemn covenant between God and your soul.

Set apart some time, more than once, to be spent in secret before the Lord – in seeking earnestly His special assistance and gracious acceptance of you – in searching your heart, whether you are sincerely willing to forsake all your sins, and to resign yourself, body and soul, unto God and His service; to serve Him in holiness and righteousness all the days of your life.

Compose your spirit into the most serious frame possible, suitable to a transaction of so high importance. Lay hold on the covenant of God, and rely on His promise of giving grace and strength, by which you may be enabled to perform your promise. Do not trust to your own strength, to the strength of your own resolutions; but take hold on His strength.

Being thus prepared, on some convenient time set apart for the purpose, enter upon the work, and solemnly, as in the presence of the Lord, fall down on your knees and spreading forth your hands towards heaven open your heart to the Lord in these, or the like words:

'O most holy God, for the passion of Thy Son, I beseech Thee accept Thy poor prodigal now prostrating himself at Thy door. I have fallen from Thee by mine iniquity, and am by nature a son of death, and a thousandfold more the child of hell by wicked practice. But of Thine infinite grace Thou hast promised mercy to me in Christ, if I will but turn to Thee with all my heart.

Therefore upon the call of Thy gospel, I am now come in, and throwing down my weapons, submit myself to Thy mercy. And because Thou requirest, as the condition of my peace with Thee, that I should put away my idols, and be at defiance with all Thine enemies, which I acknowledge I have wickedly sided with against Thee, I here from the bottom of my heart renounce them all, firmly covenanting with Thee, not to allow myself in any known sin, but conscientiously to use all the means that I know Thou hast prescribed for the death and utter destruction of all my corruptions. And whereas formerly I have inordinately and idolatrously set my affections upon the world, I do here resign my heart to Thee who madest it, humbly declaring before Thy glorious Majesty, that it is the firm resolution of my heart, and that I do unfeignedly desire grace from Thee, that when Thou shalt call me hereunto, I may practise this my resolution through Thy assistance, to forsake all that is dear unto me in this world, rather than to turn from Thee to the ways of sin; and that I will watch against all its temptations, whether of prosperity or adversity, lest they should withdraw my heart from Thee. I beseech Thee also to help me against the temptations of Satan, to whose wicked suggestions I resolve by Thy grace never to yield myself a servant. And because my own righteousness is but as filthy rags, I renounce all my confidence therein, and acknowledge that I am of myself a hopeless, helpless, undone creature, without righteousness or strength.

'And forasmuch as Thou hast of Thy bottomless mercy offered most graciously to me, a wretched sinner, to be again my God through Christ, if I would accept Thee; I call upon heaven and earth to record this day, that I do here solemnly avouch Thee for the Lord my God, and with all possible veneration, bowing the neck of my soul under the feet of Thy most sacred Majesty, I do here take Thee the Lord Jehovah, Father, Son, and Holy Ghost, for my portion and chief good, and do give myself, body and soul, to be Thy servant, promising and vowing to serve Thee in holiness and righteousness all the days of my life.

'And since Thou hast appointed the Lord Jesus Christ the only means of coming unto Thee, I do here solemnly join myself in a marriage covenant to Him.

'O Blessed Jesus, I come to Thee hungry and thirsty, poor and wretched, miserable, blind and naked, a most loathsome polluted wretch, a guilty condemned malefactor, unworthy to wash the feet of the servants of my Lord, much more to be solemnly married to the King of Glory. But such is Thine unparalleled love, I do here with all my power accept Thee, and do take Thee for my Head and Husband, for better, for worse, for richer, for poorer, for all times and conditions, to love, honour and obey Thee before all others, and this to the death. I embrace Thee in all Thine offices. I renounce my own worthiness, and do here avow Thee to be the Lord my Righteousness. I renounce my own wisdom, and do here take Thee for my only Guide. I renounce my own will, and take Thy will for my law.

'And since Thou hast told me that I must suffer if I will reign, I do here covenant with Thee to take my lot, as it falls, with Thee, and by Thy grace assisting to run all hazards with Thee, verily supposing that neither life nor death shall part between Thee and me.

'And because Thou hast been pleased to give me Thy holy laws, as the rule of my life, and the way in which I should walk to Thy kingdom, I do here willingly put my neck under Thy yoke, and set my shoulder to Thy burden; and subscribing to all Thy laws as holy, just, and good, I solemnly take them as the rule of my words, thoughts, and actions; promising that though my flesh contradict and rebel, yet I will endeavour to order and govern my whole life to Thy direction, and will not allow myself to neglect anything that I know to be my duty.

'Only because through the frailty of my flesh, I am subject to many failings, I am bold humbly to request, that unintentional shortcomings, contrary to the settled bent and resolution of my heart, shall not make void this covenant, for so Thou hast said.

'Now, Almighty God, Searcher of hearts, Thou knowest that

I make this covenant with Thee this day, without any known guile or reservation, beseeching Thee, that if Thou espiest any flaw or falsehood therein, Thou wouldst reveal it to me, and help me to do it aright.

'And now, O God the Father, whom I shall be bold from this day forward to look upon as my God and Father, glory be to Thee for finding out such a way for the recovery of undone sinners. Glory be to Thee, O God the Son, who hast loved me and washed me from my sins in Thine own blood, and art now become my Saviour and Redeemer. Glory be to Thee, O God the Holy Ghost, who by the finger of Thine almighty power hast turned about my heart from sin to God.

'O high and holy Jehovah, the Lord God Omnipotent, Father, Son, and Holy Ghost, Thou art now become my covenant Friend, and I through Thine infinite grace am become Thy covenant servant. Amen, so be it. And the covenant which I have made on earth, let it be ratified in heaven.'

This covenant I advise you to make, not only in heart, but in word; not only in word, but in writing; and that you would with all possible reverence spread the writing before the Lord, as if you would present it to Him as your Act and Deed. And when you have done this, set your hand to it and sign it. Keep it as a memorial of the solemn transactions that have passed between God and you, that you may have recourse to it in doubts and temptations.

11: Take heed of delaying your conversion, but make a speedy, an immediate surrender of your heart to God.

'*I made haste, and delayed not*' (Ps cxix 60). Remember and tremble at the sad instance of the foolish virgins who did not come till the door of mercy was shut, and of a convinced Felix who put off Paul to another season, but we do not find that he had another season. O come in while it is called to-day, lest you should be hardened through the deceitfulness of sin; lest the day of grace should be over, and the things which belong to your peace should be hid from your eyes. Now mercy is wooing you; now Christ is waiting to be gracious to you, and the Spirit of God is striving with you. Now ministers are calling; now conscience is stirring; now the market is open, and oil may be had, you have opportunity for the buying. Now Christ is to be had for the taking. Oh! strike in with the offers of grace. Oh! now, or never. If you make light of this offer, God may swear in His wrath that you shall never taste of His supper (Lk xiv 24).

12: Attend conscientiously upon the Word, as the means appointed for your conversion.

Attend, I say, not customarily, but conscientiously, with this desire, design, hope, and expectation, that you may be converted by it. Come to every sermon you hear with this thought: 'O I hope God will now come in; I hope this day may be the time, this may be the man by whom God will bring me home.' When you are coming to the privileges of God's house, lift up your heart to God thus: 'Lord, let this be the Sabbath, let this be the season in which I may receive renewing grace. O let it be said that this day such a one was born unto Thee.'

Objection. You will say, I have been a hearer of the Word a long time, yet it has not been effectual to my conversion.

Answer. Yes; but you have not attended upon it in this manner, as a means of your conversion, nor with this design, nor praying for and expecting the happy effect from it.

13: Strike in with the Spirit when He begins to work upon your heart.

When He works convictions, O do not stifle them, but join in with Him, and beg the Lord to give you saving conversion. '*Quench not the Spirit.*' Do not reject Him, do not resist Him. Beware of stifling convictions with evil company or worldly business. When you are in anguish on account of sin and fears about your eternal state, beg of God that you may have peace only in thoroughly renouncing all sin, loathing it in your inmost soul, and giving your whole heart, without reserve, to Christ. Say to Him, 'Strike home, Lord; do not leave the work half-done. Go to the bottom of my corruption, and let out the life-blood of my sins.' Thus yield yourself to the working of the Spirit, and hoist your sails to His gusts.

14: Set upon the constant and diligent use of serious and fervent prayer.

He that neglects prayer is a profane and unsanctified sinner. He that is not constant in prayer is a hypocrite, unless the omission be contrary to his ordinary course, under the force of some instant temptation. One of the first things conversion appears in is that it sets men a-praying. Therefore set to this duty. Let not one day pass in which you have not, morning and evening, set apart some time for solemn prayer in secret. Also, call your family together daily and duly to worship God with you. Woe be unto you, if you be found among the families that call not upon God's name (Jer x 25). But cold and lifeless devotions will not reach halfway to heaven. Be fervent and importunate. Importunity will carry it; but without violence the kingdom of heaven will not be taken. You must strive to enter, and wrestle with tears and supplications as Jacob, if you would gain the blessing. You are undone for ever without grace, and therefore you must set to it, and resolve to take no denial. That man who is fixed in this resolution says, 'Well, I must have grace, or I will never give over till I have grace; I will never cease earnestly pleading, and striving with God and my own heart, till He renews me by the power of His grace.'

15: Forsake your evil company, and forbear the occasions of sin.

You will never be turned from sin till you decline and forego the temptations of sin. I never expect your conversion from sin, unless you are brought to some self-denial, so as to flee the occasions. If you will be nibbling at the bait, and playing on the brink, and tampering with the snare, your soul will surely be taken. Where God exposes men, in His providence, unavoidably to temptation, and the occasions are such as we cannot remove, we may expect special assistance in the use of His means; but when we tempt God by running into danger, He will not engage to support us when we are tempted. And, of all temptations, one of the most fatal and pernicious is evil companions. O what hopeful beginnings have these often stifled! O the souls, the estates, the families, the towns, that these have ruined! How many poor sinners have been enlightened and convinced, and been just ready to escape the snare of the devil, and have even escaped it: and yet wicked company has pulled them back at last, and made them sevenfold more the children of hell! In a word, I have no hopes of you, except you shake off your evil company. Your life depends upon it: forsake this, or you cannot live. Will you be worse than the ass of Balaam, to run on when you see the Lord with a drawn sword in the way? Let this sentence be written in capitals upon your conscience, 'A COMPANION OF FOOLS SHALL BE DESTROYED' (Prov xiii 20). The Lord has spoken it, and who shall reverse it?

And will you run upon destruction when God Himself forewarns you? If God ever changes your heart, it will appear in the change of your company. O fear and flee the gulf by which so many thousands have been swallowed up in perdition. It will be hard for you indeed to make your escape. Your companions will be mocking you out of your religion, and will study to fill you with prejudices against strictness, as ridiculous and comfortless. They will be flattering you and alluring you; but remember the warnings of the Holy Ghost: '*My son, if sinners entice thee, consent thou not. If they say, Come with us, cast in thy lot among us; walk thou not in the way with them, refrain thy foot from their path; avoid it, pass not by it, turn from it, and pass away. For the way of the wicked is as darkness, they know not at what they stumble. They lie in wait for their own blood, they lurk privily for their own lives*' (Prov i 10–19, iv 15–19). My soul is moved within me to see how many of my hearers and readers are likely to perish, both they and their houses, by this wretched mischief, even the frequenting of such places and company, by which they are drawn into sin. Once more I admonish you, as Moses did Israel, '*Depart, I pray you, from the tents of these wicked men*' (Num xvi 26). O flee from them as you would those that had the plague – sores running in their foreheads. These are the devil's panders and decoys; and if you do not make your escape they will draw you into perdition, and will prove your eternal ruin.

16: Set apart a day to humble your soul in secret by fasting and prayer, to work a sense of your sins and miseries upon your heart.
Read over a thorough exposition of the Commandments, and write down the duties omitted, and sins committed by you against every commandment, and so make a catalogue of your sins, and with shame and sorrow spread them before the Lord. And if your heart be truly willing to the terms, join yourself solemnly to the Lord in that covenant set down in Direction 10 of this chapter, and the Lord grant you mercy in His sight.

Thus, I have told you what you must do to be saved. Will you now obey the voice of the Lord? Will you arise and set to the work? O man, what answer will you make, what excuse will you have, if you should perish at last through very wilfulness, when you have known the way of life? I do not fear your miscarrying, if your own idleness do not at last undo you, in neglecting the use of the means that are so plainly here prescribed. Rouse up, O sluggard, and ply your work. Be doing, and the Lord will be with you.

A SHORT SOLILOQUY
FOR AN UNREGENERATE SINNER

Ah! wretched man that I am! What a condition have I brought myself into by sin! Oh! I see my heart has deceived me all this while, in flattering me that my condition was good. I see, I see, I am but a lost and undone man, for ever undone, unless the

Lord help me out of this condition. My sins! My sins! Lord, what an unclean, polluted wretch I am! More loathsome and odious to Thee than the most hateful venom or noisome carcase can be to me. Oh! what a hell of sin is in this heart of mine, which I have flattered myself to be a good heart! Lord, how universally am I corrupted, in all my parts, powers, performances! All the imaginations of my heart are only evil continually. I am under an inability to, and aversion from, and an enmity against anything that is good; and am prone to all that is evil. My heart is a very sink of sin: and oh the innumerable hosts and swarms of sinful thoughts, words and actions that have flowed from it! Oh the load of guilt that is on my soul! My head is full, and my heart is full; my mind and my members, they are all full of sin. Oh my sins! How do they stare upon me! Woe is me, my creditors are upon me: every commandment takes hold upon me, for more than ten thousand talents, yes, ten thousand times ten thousand. How endless then is the sum of all my debts! If this whole world were filled up from earth to heaven with paper, and all this paper written over within and without by arithmeticians, yet, when all were added up, it would come inconceivably short of what I owe to the least of God's commandments. Woe unto me, for my debts are infinite, and my sins are increased. They are wrongs to an infinite Majesty, and if he that commits treason against a silken mortal is worthy to be racked, drawn and quartered; what have I deserved that have so often lifted up my hand against Heaven, and have struck at the crown and dignity of the Almighty?

Oh my sins! my sins! Behold, a troop comes! Multitudes! multitudes! there is no number of their armies. Innumerable evils have compassed me about; mine iniquities have taken hold upon me; they have set themselves against me. Oh! it were better to have all the regiments of hell come against me, than to have my sins fall upon me, to the spoiling of my soul. Lord, how am I surrounded! How many are they that rise up against me! They have beset me behind and before; they swarm within me and without me; they have possessed all my powers, and have fortified my unhappy soul as a garrison, which this brood of hell mans and maintains against the God that made me.

And they are as mighty as they are many. The sands are many, but then they are not great: the mountains great but then they are not many. But woe is me, my sins are as many as the sands, and as mighty as the mountains. Their weight is greater than their number. It were better that the rocks and the mountains should fall upon me, than the crushing and unsupportable load of my own sins. Lord, I am heavy laden; let mercy help, or I am gone. Unload me of this heavy guilt, this sinking load, or I am crushed without hope, and must be pressed down to hell. If my grief were thoroughly weighed, and my sins laid in the balance together, they would be heavier than the sand of the sea; therefore my words are swallowed up: they would weigh down all the rocks and the hills, and turn the balance against all the isles of the earth. O Lord, Thou knowest my manifold transgressions, and my mighty sins.

Ah, my soul! Alas, my glory! How are you humbled! Once the glory of the creation, and the image of God: now, a lump of filthiness, a coffin of rottenness, replenished with stench and loathsomeness. Oh what work has sin made with you! You shall be termed 'Forsaken' and all the rooms of your faculties 'Desolate', and the name that you shall be called by is 'Ichabod', or, 'Where is the glory?' How are you come down mightily! My beauty is turned into deformity, and my glory into shame. Lord, what a loathsome leper am I! The ulcerous bodies of Job or Lazarus were not more offensive to the eyes and nostrils of men, than I must needs be to the most holy God, whose eyes cannot behold iniquity.

And what misery have my sins brought upon me! Lord, what a state I am in! Sold under sin, cast out of God's favour, accursed from the Lord, cursed in my body, cursed in my soul, cursed in my name, in my estate, my relations, and all that I have. My sins are unpardoned, and my soul within a step of death. Alas! what shall I do? Where shall I go? Which way shall I look? God is frowning on me from above, hell gaping for me beneath, conscience smiting me within, temptations and dangers surrounding me without. Oh, where shall I fly? What place can hide me from Omniscience? What power can secure me from Omnipotence?

What do you mean, O my soul, to go on thus? Are you in league with hell? Have you made a covenant with death? Are you in love with your misery? Is it good for you to be here? Alas, what shall I do? Shall I go on in my sinful ways? Why then, certain damnation will be my end; and shall I be so besotted and mad as to go and sell my soul to the flames, for a little ale, or a little ease, for a little pleasure or gain or comfort to my flesh? Shall I linger any longer in this wretched state? No: if I tarry here I shall die. What then, is there no help? No hope? None, except I turn. Why, but is there any remedy for such woeful misery? Any mercy after such provoking iniquity? Yes: as sure as God's oath is true, I shall have pardon and mercy yet, if I presently, unfeignedly, and unreservedly turn by Christ to Him.

Why then, I thank Thee upon the bended knees of my soul, O most merciful Jehovah, that Thy patience has waited for me hitherto; for hadst Thou taken me away in this state, I had perished for ever. And now I adore Thy grace, and accept the offers of Thy mercy, I renounce all my sins, and resolve by Thy grace to set myself against them, and to follow Thee in holiness and righteousness all the days of my life.

Who am I, Lord, that I should make any claim to Thee, or have any part or portion in Thee, who am not worthy to lick up the dust of Thy feet? Yet since Thou holdest forth the golden sceptre, I am bold to come and touch. To despair would be to disparage Thy mercy; and to stand off when Thou biddest me come would be at once to undo myself and rebel against Thee under pretence of humility. Therefore I bow my soul unto Thee, and with all possible thankfulness accept Thee as mine, and give up myself to Thee as Thine. Thou shalt be Sovereign over me, my King, and my God. Thou shalt be on the throne, and all my powers shall bow to Thee, they shall come and worship before

Thy feet. Thou shalt be my portion, O Lord, and I will rest in Thee.

Thou callest for my heart. Oh that it were any way fit for Thine acceptance! I am unworthy, O Lord, everlastingly unworthy to be Thine. But since Thou wilt have it so, I freely give my heart to Thee. Take it, it is Thine. Oh that it were better! But Lord, I put it into Thy hands, who alone canst mend it. Mould it after Thine own heart; make it as Thou wouldst have it, holy, humble, heavenly, soft, tender, flexible, and write Thy law upon it.

Come, Lord Jesus, come quickly. Enter in triumphantly. Take me up for Thyself for ever. I give myself to Thee, I come to Thee, as the only way to the Father, as the only Mediator, the means ordained to bring me to God. I have destroyed myself, but in Thee is my help. Save, Lord, or else I perish. I come to Thee, with the rope about my neck. I am worthy to die and to be damned. Never was the hire more due to the servant, never was penny more due to the labourer, than death and hell, my just wages, are due to me for my sins. But I fly to Thy merits; I trust alone to the value and virtue of Thy sacrifice, and prevalence of Thy intercession. I submit to Thy teaching, I make choice of Thy government. Stand open, ye everlasting doors, that the King of Glory may enter in.

O Thou Spirit of the Most High, the Comforter and Sanctifier of Thy chosen, come in with all Thy glorious train, all Thy courtly attendants, Thy fruits and graces. Let me be Thine habitation. I can give Thee but what is Thine own already; but here with the widow I give my two mites, my soul and my body, into Thy treasury, fully resigning them up to Thee, to be sanctified by Thee, to be servants to Thee. They shall be Thy patients; cure Thou their maladies. They shall be Thy agents; govern Thou their actions. Too long have I served the world; too long have I hearkened to Satan; but now I renounce them all, and will be ruled by Thy dictates and directions, and guided by Thy counsel.

O blessed Trinity, O glorious Unity, I deliver myself up to

Thee. Receive me: write Thy name, O Lord, upon me, and upon all that I have, as Thy proper goods. Set Thy mark upon me, upon every member of my body, and every faculty of my soul. I have chosen Thy precepts. Thy law will I lay before me; this shall be the copy which I will keep in my eye, and study to write after. According to this rule do I resolve by Thy grace to walk: after this law shall my whole man be governed. And though I cannot perfectly keep one of Thy commandments, yet I will allow myself in the breach of none. I know my flesh will hang back: but I resolve, in the power of Thy grace, to cleave to Thee and Thy holy ways, whatever it cost me. I am sure I cannot come off a loser by Thee: and therefore I will be content with reproach, and difficulties and hardships here, and will deny myself, and take up Thy cross, and follow Thee. Lord Jesus, Thy yoke is easy, Thy cross is welcome, as it is the way to Thee. I lay aside all hopes of a worldly happiness. I will be content to tarry till I come to Thee. Let me be poor and low, little and despised here, so I may be but admitted to live and reign with Thee hereafter. Lord, Thou hast my heart and hand to this agreement. Be it as the laws of the Medes and Persians, never to be reversed. To this I will stand: in this resolution, by Thy grace, I will live and die. I have sworn, and will perform it, that I will keep Thy righteous judgments. I have given my free consent, I have made my everlasting choice. Lord Jesus, confirm the contract. Amen.

7

The motives to conversion

Though what has already been said of the necessity of conversion and of the miseries of the unconverted might be sufficient to induce any considerate mind to resolve upon a present turning to God; yet, knowing what a piece of desperate obstinacy and untractableness the heart of man naturally is, I have thought it necessary to add some motives to persuade you to be reconciled to God.

'O Lord, do not fail me now, at my last attempts. If any soul has read hitherto, and is yet untouched, Lord, fasten on him now, and do Thy work. Take him by the heart, overcome him, persuade him, till he say, "Thou hast prevailed, for Thou art stronger than I." Lord, didst not Thou make me a fisher of men, and have I toiled all this while and caught nothing? Alas, that I should have spent my strength for naught! and now I am casting my last. Lord Jesus, stand Thou upon the shore, and direct how and where I shall spread my net; and let me so enclose with arguments the souls I seek, that they may not be able to get out. Now, Lord, for a multitude of souls; now for a full draught. O Lord God, remember me, I pray Thee, and strengthen me this once, O God.'

Men and brethren, heaven and earth call upon you; yea, hell itself preaches the doctrine of repentance unto you. The ministers of the churches labour for you. The angels of heaven wait for you, for your repenting and turning unto God. O sinner, why should devils laugh at your destruction, and deride your misery, and sport themselves with your folly? This will be your case, except you turn. And were it not better you should be a joy to

The motives to conversion

angels than a laughing-stock and sport for devils. Verily, if you would but come in, the heavenly hosts would take up their anthems and sing, 'Glory to God in the highest'; the morning stars would sing together, and all the sons of God shout for joy, and celebrate this new creation as they did the first. Your repentance would, as it were, make a holiday in heaven, and the glorious spirits would rejoice, in that there is a new brother added to their society, another heir born to the Lord, and a lost son received safe and sound. The true penitent's tears are indeed the wine that maketh glad both God and man.

If it be little that men and angels would rejoice at your conversion, know also that God Himself would rejoice over you, even with singing (Lk xv 9; Is lxii 5). Never did Jacob with such joy weep over the neck of his Joseph, as your heavenly Father would rejoice over you upon your coming to Him. Look over the story of the Prodigal Son. I think I see how the aged father lays aside his state and forgets his years; behold, how he runs. O the haste that mercy makes: the sinner makes not half that speed. I think I see how his heart moves, how his compassions yearn. How quick-sighted is love! Mercy spies him a great way off; forgets his riotous course, unnatural rebellion, horrid unthankfulness – not a word of these – and receives him with open arms, clasps him about his neck, kisses him; calls for the fatted calf, the best robe, the ring, the shoes, the best cheer in heaven's store, the best attire in heaven's wardrobe. Yea, the joy cannot be held in his own breast. Others must be called to participate. The friends sympathise; but none know the joy the father has in his new-born son, whom he has received from the dead. I think I hear the music at a distance. O the melody of the heavenly choristers! I cannot learn the song (Rev xiv 3) but I think I overhear the theme at which all the harmonious choir with one consent strike sweetly in: 'For this my son was dead, and is alive again; he was lost, and is found.' I need not explain the parable further. God is the father: Christ is the provision, His righteousness the robe, His grace the ornaments, ministers, saints and angels, the friends and servants, and you that read, if you will but unfeignedly repent and turn, the welcome prodigal, the happy instance of this grace, the blessed subject of this joy and love.

O rock! O adamant! What, not moved yet? Not yet resolved to turn forthwith and to close with mercy? I will try yet once again. If one were sent to you from the dead, would you be persuaded? Why, hear the voice from the dead, from the damned, crying to you that you should repent: '*I pray thee that thou wouldest send him to my father's house; for I have five brethren; that he may testify to them, lest they also come into this place of torment; if one went to them from the dead, they will repent*' (Lk xvi 27–28). Hear, O man; your predecessors in impenitence preach to you from the infernal flames, that you should repent. O look down into the bottomless pit. Do you see how the smoke of their torment ascendeth for ever and ever? What do you think of those chains of darkness? Can you be content to burn? Do you see how the worm gnaws, how the fire rages? What do you say to that gulf of perdition? Will you take up your habitation there? O lay your ear to the door of hell. Do you hear the curses and blasphemies, the weepings and wailings, how they lament their follies and curse their day? How do they roar and gnash their teeth! how deep their groans! how inconceivable their miseries! If the shrieks of Korah, Dathan, and Abiram, were so terrible when the earth clave asunder and opened its mouth and swallowed them up, and all that appertained to them, that all Israel fled at the cry of them (Num xvi 33–34), O how fearful would the cry be if God should take off the covering from the mouth of hell, and let the cry of the damned ascend in all its terror among the children of men! And of their moans and miseries this is the piercing, killing emphasis and burden, 'For ever! for ever!'

As God liveth that made your soul, you are but a few hours distant from all this, except you be converted.

O! I am even lost and swallowed up in the abundance of those arguments that I might suggest. If there be any point of wisdom in all the world, it is to repent and come in. If there be anything righteous, anything reasonable, this is it. If there be anything that may be called madness and folly, and anything that may be counted sottish, absurd, brutish, and unreasonable, it is this, to go on in your unconverted state. Let me beg of you, as you would not willingly destroy yourself, sit down and weigh, besides what has been said, these following motives, and let conscience say if it be not most reasonable that you should repent and turn.

1: The God that made you most graciously invites you.

His most sweet and merciful nature invites you. O the kindness of God, His boundless compassion, His tender mercies! As the heavens are higher than the earth, so are His ways above our ways, and His thoughts above our thoughts. *'He is full of compassion, and gracious, long-suffering, and plenteous in mercy'* (Ps lxxxvi 15). This is a great argument to persuade sinners to come. *'Turn unto the Lord; for He is gracious and merciful, slow to anger, of great kindness, and repenteth him of the evil.'* If God would not repent of the evil, it would be some discouragement to our repenting. If there were no hope of mercy, it would be no wonder that rebels should stand out; but never had subjects such a gracious prince, such pity, patience, and clemency to deal with, as you have. *'Who is a God like unto Thee, that pardoneth iniquity?'* (Micah vii 18). O sinners, see what a God you have to deal with. If you will but turn, *'he will turn again, and have compassion on you; he will subdue your iniquities, and cast all your sins into the depths of the sea'.* *'Return unto me, saith the Lord of hosts, and I will return unto you'* (Mal iii 7). Sinners do not fail in that they have too high thoughts of God's mercies, but in that they overlook His justice, or they promise themselves mercy out of God's way. His mercies are beyond all imagination; great mercies, manifold mercies (Neh ix 19), tender mercies, sure mercies, everlasting mercies; and all is yours, if you will but turn. Are you willing to come in? The Lord has laid aside His terror and erected a throne of grace. He holds forth the golden sceptre: touch and live. Would a merciful man slay his enemy when prostrate at his feet, acknowledging his wrong, begging pardon, and offering to enter with him into a covenant of peace? Much less will the merciful God. Study His name (Ex xxxiv 7), '*Keeping mercy for thousands, forgiving iniquity and transgression and sin.*' Also read experience, Neh ix 17.

God's soul-encouraging calls and promises invite you. Ah, what an earnest suitor is mercy to you! How lovingly, how instantly, it calls after you! How earnestly it woos you! '*Return thou backsliding Israel, saith the Lord, and I will not cause my anger to fall upon you; for I am merciful, saith the Lord, and I will not keep anger for ever; only acknowledge thine iniquity. Turn, O backsliding children, saith the Lord; return, and I will heal thy backslidings. Thou hast played the harlot with many lovers; yet return unto me, saith the Lord*' (Jer iii). '*As I live, saith the Lord God, I have no pleasure in the death of the wicked, but that he turn from his way and live. Turn ye, turn ye from your evil ways; for why will ye die, O house of Israel?*' (Ezek xxxiii 11). '*If the wicked will turn from all his sins that he hath committed, and keep all my statutes, and do that which is lawful and right, he shall surely live, he shall not die. All the transgressions that he hath committed, they shall not be mentioned unto him; in his righteousness that he hath done, he shall live. . . . Repent, and turn you from all your transgressions; so iniquity shall not be your ruin. Cast away from you all your transgressions, and make you a new heart and a new spirit; for why will ye die, O Israel? For I have no pleasure in the death of him that dieth, saith the Lord God, wherefore turn yourselves, and live ye*' (Ezek xviii).

O melting, gracious words: the voice of God, and not of a man! This is not the manner of men, for the offended sovereign to sue to the offending, traitorous rebel. O how does mercy follow you, and plead with you! Is not your heart broken yet? O that today you would hear His voice!

2: The doors of heaven are thrown open to you.

The everlasting gates are set wide open for you, and an

abundant entrance into the kingdom of heaven is administered to you.

Christ now addresses you, and calls upon you to arise and take possession of this good land. View the glory of the other world, as set forth in the map of the gospel. Get up into the Pisgah of the promises, and lift up your eyes northward, and southward, and eastward, and westward, and see the good land that is beyond Jordan, and that goodly mountain. Behold the Paradise of God, watered with the streams of glory. Arise and walk through the land, in the length of it, and in the breadth of it; for the land which you see, the Lord will give it to you for ever, if you will but return. Let me say to you, as Paul to Agrippa, 'Believest thou the prophets?' If you believe indeed, view what glorious things are spoken of the city of God, and know that all this is here tendered in the name of God to you. As verily as God is true, it shall be for ever yours, if you will but thoroughly turn.

Behold the city of pure transparent gold, whose foundations are garnished with all manner of precious stones, whose gates are pearls, whose light is glory, whose temple is God. Believest thou this? If you do, are you not beside yourself, that will not take possession when the gates are thrown open to you, and you are bidden to enter? O ye sons of folly, will you embrace the dunghill and refuse the kingdom? Behold, the Lord takes you up into the mountain, shows you the kingdom of heaven and all the glory thereof, and tells you, 'All this will I give you, if you will fall down and worship me; if you will submit to mercy, accept my Son, and serve me in righteousness and holiness.' 'O fools and slow of heart to believe!' Will you seek and serve the world, and neglect eternal glory? What! not enter into paradise when the flaming sword, which was once set to keep you out, is now used to drive you in? But you will say I am uncharitable to think you infidels and unbelievers. What, then, shall I think of you? Either you are desperate unbelievers that do not credit it; or beside yourselves, that you know and believe the excellence and eternity of this glory, and yet do so fearfully neglect it.

Do but attend to what is offered you: a blessed kingdom, a kingdom of glory, a kingdom of righteousness, a kingdom of peace, and an everlasting kingdom. Here you shall dwell, here you shall reign for ever, and the Lord shall seat you on a throne of glory, and with His own hand shall set the royal diadem upon your head, and give you a crown – not of thorns, for there shall be no sinning nor suffering there: not of gold, for this shall be viler than the dirt in that day; but a crown of life, a crown of righteousness, a crown of glory, yea, you shall put on glory as a robe, and shall shine like the sun in the firmament of your Father. Look now on your worthless flesh. This flesh, which is mere dust and ashes, shall be brighter than the stars. In short, you shall be made like unto the angels of God and behold His face in righteousness. Look now and tell me, do you not yet believe? If not, conscience must pronounce you an infidel; for it is the very word of God that I speak.

But if you say you believe, let me next know your resolution. Will you embrace this for your happiness? Will you forgo your sinful gains, your forbidden pleasures? Will you trample on the world's esteem, and stop your ears to its flatteries, and wrest yourself out of its embraces? Will you be content to take up with reproach and poverty, if they lie in the way to heaven, and follow the Lord with humble self-denial, in a mortified and flesh-displeasing life? If so, all is yours, and that for ever.

And is not the offer a fair one? Is it not just that he should be damned that will go on and perish, when all this may be had by taking it? Will you not take God at His word? Will you not let go your hold of the world, and lay hold on eternal life? If not, let conscience tell you whether you are not beside yourself, that you should neglect so happy a choice, by which you might be made happy for ever.

3: God will give you unspeakable privileges in this life.

Though the fullness of your blessedness shall be reserved till hereafter, yet God will give you no little things in hand. He will redeem you from your thraldom. He will pluck you from the paw of the lion. The serpent shall bruise your heel, but you shall bruise his head. He shall deliver you from this present evil world. Prosperity shall not destroy you; adversity shall not separate Him and you. He will redeem you from the power of the grave, and make the king of terrors a messenger of peace to you. He will take out the curse from the cross, and make affliction the refining-pot to purify the metal, the fan to blow off the chaff, the medicine to cure the mind. He will save you from the arrest of the law, and turn the curse into a blessing to you. He has the keys of hell and of death, and shutteth and no man openeth, and He will shut its mouth, as once He did the lions', that you shall not be hurt of the second death.

Besides, He will not only save from misery, but install you into unspeakable prerogatives. He will bestow Himself upon you; He will be a Friend and a Father unto you. He will be a Sun and a Shield to you. In a word, He will be a God to you. And what more can be said? What may you expect that a God should do for you, and be to you? *That* He will be, *that* He will do. She that marries a prince expects he should do for her like a prince, that she may live in suitable state, and have an answerable dowry. He that has a king for his father or a friend, expects he should do for him like a king. Alas, the kings and monarchs of the earth, so much above you, are but like the painted butterflies amongst the rest of their kind, or the fair coloured palmerworm amongst the rest of the worms, if compared with God. As He infinitely exceeds the glory and power of His glittering dust, so He will, beyond all proportion, exceed in doing for His favourites whatever princes can do for theirs. He will give you grace and glory, and withhold no good thing from you. He will take you for His sons and daughters, and make you heirs of His promises, and establish His everlasting covenant with you. He will justify you from all that law, conscience and Satan can charge upon you. He will give you free access into His presence, and accept your person, and receive your prayers. He will abide in you, and hold a constant and friendly communion with you. His ear shall be open, His door open, His store open, at all times to you. His blessing shall rest upon you, and He will make your enemies serve you, and work out all things for good unto you.

4: The terms of mercy are brought as low as possible to you.

God has stooped as low to sinners as with honour He can. He will not be the author of sin, nor stain the glory of His holiness; and how could He come lower than He has, unless He should do this?

God does not impose anything unreasonable or impossible, as a condition of life, upon you. Two things were necessary to be done, according to the tenor of the first covenant. 1. That we should fully satisfy the demands of justice for past offences. 2. That we should perform personally, perfectly, and perpetually, the whole law for the time to come. By our sins we render salvation through either of these ways impossible. But behold God's gracious provision in both. He does not insist upon satisfaction: He is content to take of the Surety, and He of His own providing too, what He might have exacted from you. '*All things are of God, who hath reconciled us to himself by Jesus Christ, and hath given to us the ministry of reconciliation: to wit, that God was in Christ reconciling the world unto himself, not imputing their trespasses unto them; and hath committed unto us the word of reconciliation*' (2 Cor v 18-19). He declares Himself to have received a ransom, and that He expects nothing but that you should accept His Son, and He shall be righteousness and redemption to you. If you come in His Christ, and set your heart to please Him, making this your chief concern, He will graciously accept you.

O consider the condescension of your God! Let me say to you, as Naaman's servant to him, '*My father, if the prophet had bid thee do some great thing, wouldest thou not have done it? How much rather when he saith to thee, Wash and be clean!*' If God demanded some terrible, some severe and rigorous thing of you, to escape eternal damnation, would you not have done it? Suppose it had been to spend all your days in sorrow in some howling wilderness, or pine with famine, would you not have thankfully accepted eternal redemption, though these had been the conditions? Nay, farther, if God had told you that you should burn in the fire for millions of ages, or be so long tormented in hell, would you not have accepted it? Alas, all these are not so much as one grain of sand in the glass of eternity. If your offended Creator should have held you but one year upon the rack, and then bid you come and forsake your sins, accept Christ, and serve him a few years in self-denial or lie in this case for ever and ever; do you think you should have hesitated at the offer, and disputed the terms, and have been unresolved whether to accept the proposal? O sinner, return and live; why should you die when life is to be had for the taking, when mercy entreats you to be saved? Could you say, 'Lord, I knew thee, that thou wast a hard man', even then you would have no excuse; but when the God of Heaven has stooped so low, and condescended so far, if still you stand off, who shall plead for you?

Objection: Notwithstanding all the advantages of the new covenant, I am unable to repent and believe, and so comply with its conditions.

Answer: These you may perform by God's grace enabling; but let the next consideration serve for a fuller answer.

5: God offers all needed grace to enable you.

'*I have stretched out mine hand, and no man regarded*' (Prov i 24). What though you are plunged into the ditch of that misery from which you can never get out? Christ offers to help you out; He reaches out His hand to you; and if you perish, it is for refusing His help. '*Behold, I stand at the door and knock; if any man open to me, I will come in.*' (Rev iii 20). What though you are poor, and wretched, and blind, and naked? Christ offers a cure for your blindness, a covering for your nakedness, riches for your poverty. He tenders you His righteousness, His grace:

'*I counsel thee to buy of me gold, that thou mayest be rich; and white raiment, that thou mayest be clothed; and anoint thy eyes with eyesalve, that thou mayest see.*' Do you say, 'The condition is impossible; for I have nothing with which to buy?' You must know that this buying is '*without money and without price.*' This buying is by begging and seeking with your whole heart. God commands you to know Him, and to fear Him. Do you say, 'Yes, but my mind is blinded, and my heart is hardened from His fear?' I answer that God offers to enlighten your mind, and to teach you His fear. So that now, if men live in ignorance and estrangement from the Lord, it is because they will not understand, and do not desire the knowledge of His ways. '*If thou criest after knowledge, if thou seekest her as silver, then shalt thou understand the fear of the Lord, and find the knowledge of God.*' (Prov ii 3–5). Is not this a fair offer? '*Turn you at my reproof; behold, I will pour out my Spirit unto you*' (Prov i 23). Though of yourselves you can do nothing, yet you may do all through His Spirit enabling you, and He offers assistance to you. God bids you '*wash and make you clean*'. You say you are unable, as much as the leopard to wash out his spots. Yes, but the Lord offers to cleanse you; so that if you are filthy still, it is through your own wilfulness: '*I have purged thee, and thou wast not purged*' (Ezek xxiv 13). '*O Jerusalem, wilt thou not be made clean: when shall it once be?*' (Jer xiii 27). God invites you to be made clean, and entreats you to yield to Him. O accept His offers, and let Him do for you, and in you, what you cannot do for yourselves.

Conclusion

And now, beloved, let me know your mind. What do you intend to do? Will you go on and die, or will you turn and lay hold on eternal life? How long will you linger in Sodom? How long will you halt between two opinions? Have you not yet resolved whether Christ or Barabbas, whether bliss or torment, whether this vain and wretched world, or the paradise of God, be the better choice? Is it a disputable case whether the Abana and Pharpar of Damascus be better than all the streams of Eden; or whether the vile pool of sin is to be preferred before the water of life, clear as crystal, proceeding out of the throne of God and of the Lamb? Can the world in good earnest do that for you which Christ can? Will it stand by you to eternity? Will pleasures, lands, titles, and treasures descend with you? If not, had you not need look after something that will? What do you mean to stand wavering? Shall I leave you at last, like Agrippa, only almost persuaded? You are for ever lost if left here; as good be not at all, as not altogether a Christian. How long will you rest in idle wishes and fruitless purposes? When will you come to a fixed, firm, and full resolve? Do you not see how Satan cheats you by tempting you to delay? How long has he drawn you on in the way of perdition!

Well, do not put me off with a dilatory answer; tell me not later. I must have your immediate consent. If you are not now resolved, while the Lord is treating with you and inviting you, much less likely are you to be later, when these impressions are worn off, and you are hardened through the deceitfulness of sin.

Will you give me your hand? Will you set open the door and give the Lord Jesus the full and ready possession? Will you put your name unto His covenant? What do you resolve upon? If you still delay, my labour is lost, and all is likely to come to nothing. Come, cast in your lot; make your choice. '*Now is the accepted time; now is the day of salvation; today, if you will hear His voice.*' Why should not this be the day from which you are able to date your happiness? Why should you venture a day longer in this dangerous and dreadful condition? What if God should this night require your soul? O that thou mightest know in this thy day the things that belong to thy peace, before they be hid from thine eyes! This is your day, and it is but a day. Others have had their day, and have received their doom; and now are you brought upon the stage of this world, here to act your part for your eternity. Remember, you are now upon your good behaviour for everlasting; if you do not make a wise choice now, you are undone for ever. What your present choice is, such must be your eternal condition.

And is it true indeed? Are life and death at your choice? Why, then, what hinders but that you should be happy? Nothing does or can hinder but your own wilful neglect or refusal. It was the saying of the eunuch to Philip, '*See, here is water, what doth hinder me to be baptized?*' So I may say to you, 'See, here is Christ, here is mercy, pardon, life; what hinders but that you should be pardoned and saved?' One of the martyrs, as he was praying at the stake, had his pardon set by him in a box, which indeed he rightly refused, because upon unworthy terms; but here the terms are most honourable and easy. O sinner, will you perish with your pardon by you? Do but henceforth give your consent to Christ, to renounce your sins, deny yourself, take up the yoke and the cross, and you carry the day. Christ is yours; pardon, peace, life, blessedness, are all yours. And is not this an offer worth embracing? Why should you hesitate or doubtfully dispute about the case? Is it not past controversy whether God be better than sin, and glory than vanity? Why should you forsake your own mercy, and sin against your own life? When will you shake off your sloth, and lay by your excuses? Boast not of tomorrow, you know not where you may lodge this night.

Now the Holy Spirit is striving with you. He will not always strive. Have you not felt your heart warmed by the Word, and been almost persuaded to leave off your sins and come to Christ? Have you not felt some motions in your mind, in which you have been warned of your danger, and told what your careless course would end in? It may be you are like young Samuel who, when the Lord called once and again, knew not the voice of the Lord, but these motions are the offers, and callings, and strivings of the Spirit. O take advantage of the tide, and know the day of your visitation.

Now the Lord Jesus stretches wide His arms to receive you. He beseeches you by us. How movingly, how meltingly, how compassionately He calls. The church is put into a sudden ecstasy at the sound of His voice, '*the voice of my beloved*'. O will you turn a deaf ear to His voice? Is it not the voice that breaks the cedars, and makes the mountains to skip like a calf; that shakes the wilderness, and divides the flames of fire? It is not Sinai's thunder, but a soft and still voice. It is not the voice of Mount Ebal, a voice of cursing and terror, but the voice of Mount Gerizim, the voice of blessing and glad tidings of good things. It is not the voice of the trumpet nor the noise of war, but a message of peace from the King of peace. I may say to you, O sinner, as Martha to her sister, '*The Master is come, and he calleth for thee.*' Now then, with Mary, arise quickly and come unto Him. How sweet are His invitations! He cries in the open concourse, '*If any man thirst, let him come unto me and drink*' (Jn vii 37). How bountiful is He! He excludes none. '*Whosoever will, let him take the water of life freely*' (Rev xxii 17). '*Come, eat of my bread, and drink of the wine that I have mingled. Forsake the foolish and live*' (Prov ix 5–6). '*Come unto me, take my yoke upon you, and learn of me, and ye shall find rest to your souls*' (Mt xi 28–29). '*Him that cometh to me, I will in no wise cast out*' (Jn vi 37).

How does He bemoan the obstinate refuser! '*O Jerusalem, Jerusalem, how often would I have gathered thy children, as a hen gathereth her chickens under her wings, and ye would not!*' (Mt xxiii 37). '*Behold me, behold me: I have stretched out my hands all the day to a rebellious people*' (Is lxv 1–2). O be persuaded now at last to throw yourselves into the arms of His love.

Behold, O ye sons of men, the Lord Jesus has thrown open the prison, and now He comes to you by His ministers, and beseeches you to come out. If it were from a palace or paradise that Christ did call you, it were no wonder that you were unwilling; and yet how easily was Adam beguiled from it; but it is from your prison, from your chains, from the dungeon, from the darkness, that He calls you, and yet will you not come? He calls you unto liberty, and yet will you not hearken? His yoke is easy, His laws are liberty, His service is freedom, and whatever prejudice you may have against His ways, if God may be believed, you shall find them all pleasure and peace, and shall taste sweetness and joy unutterable, and take infinite delight and felicity in them (Prov iii 17; 1 Pet i 8; Ps cxix 103, 111, 165).

Beloved, I am loath to leave you. I cannot tell how to give you up. I am now ready to close, but I would see a covenant made between Christ and you before I end. What! shall I leave you at last as I found you? Have you read thus far, and not yet resolved to abandon all your sins and to close with Jesus Christ? Alas, what shall I say? What shall I do? Will you turn off all my importunity? Have I run in vain? Have I used so many arguments, and spent so much time to persuade you, and must I sit down at last in disappointment? But it is a small matter that you turn me off; you put a slight upon the God that made you; you reject the compassion and beseechings of a Saviour, and will be found resisters of the Holy Ghost, if you will not now be prevailed upon to repent and be converted.

Well, though I have called you long, and you have refused, I shall yet this once more lift up my voice like a trumpet, and cry from the highest places of the city before I conclude, with the miserable exclamation, 'All is over!' Once more I shall call after regardless sinners, that, if it be possible, I may awaken them; '*O earth, earth, earth, hear the word of the Lord*' (Jer xxii 29). Unless you are resolved to die, lend your ears to the last calls of mercy. Behold, in the name of God, I make open proclamation to you, '*Hearken unto me, O ye children; hear instruction and be wise, and refuse it not*' (Prov viii 32–33).

'*Ho, every one that thirsteth, come ye to the waters; and he that hath no money, come ye, buy and eat; yea, come, buy wine and milk, without money and without price. Wherefore do ye spend money for that which is not bread, and your labour for that which satisfieth not? Hearken diligently unto me, and eat ye that which is good, and let your soul delight itself in fatness. Incline your ear and come unto me; hear, your soul shall live; and I will make an everlasting covenant with you, even the sure mercies of David*' (Is lv 1–3).

Ho, every one that is sick of any manner of disease or torment, or is possessed with an evil spirit, whether of pride, fury, lust, or covetousness, come ye to the Physician. Bring your sick. Lo, here is He that healeth all manner of sicknesses, and all manner of diseases, among the people (Mt iv 23–24).

Ho, every one that is in distress, gather yourselves unto Christ, and He will become a Captain over you. He will be your protection from the arrests of the law; He will save you from the hand of justice. Behold, He is an open sanctuary to you; He is a known refuge. Away with your sins and come in unto Him, lest the avenger of blood seize you, lest devouring wrath overtake you.

Ho, every blind and ignorant sinner, come and buy eye-salve, that you may see. Away with your excuses; you are for ever lost if you continue in this state. But accept Christ for your Prophet, and He will be a light unto you. Cry unto Him for knowledge, study His Word, take pains about religion, humble yourself before God, and He will teach you His way, and make you wise unto salvation. But if you will not follow Him, but sit down because you have but one talent, He will condemn you for a wicked and slothful servant (Mt xxv 24–26).

Ho, every profane sinner, come in and live. Return unto the Lord, and He will have mercy on you; be entreated. O return, come. You that have filled your mouth with oaths and execrations, all manner of sins and blasphemies shall be forgiven you, if you will but thoroughly turn unto Christ and come in. O unclean sinner, put away your whoredoms out of your sight, and your adulteries from between your breasts, and give yourself unto Christ, as a vessel of holiness, alone for His use; and then, '*though your sins be as scarlet, they shall be white as snow; though they be red like crimson, they shall be as wool*' (Lk vii 47; Is i 18, iv 7).

Hear, O ye drunkards, how long will you be drunk? Put away your wine. Though you have rolled in the filthiness of your sin, give yourselves unto Christ, to live soberly, righteously, and godly; embrace His righteousness; accept His government; and though you have been vile, He will wash you (Rev i 5).

Hear, O ye loose companions, whose delight is in vain and wicked society, to sport away your time in carnal mirth; come in at Wisdom's call, and choose her and her ways, and you shall live (Prov ix 5–6).

Hear, O ye scorners, hear the word of the Lord. Though you make a sport at godliness and its professors, though you have made a scorn of Christ and His ways, yet even to you does He call, to gather you under the wings of His mercy. In a word, though you should be found among the worst of that black roll, yet upon your thorough conversion you shall be washed, you shall be sanctified, you shall be justified in the name of the Lord Jesus, and by the Spirit of God (1 Cor vi 10, 11).

Ho, every formal professor, you that are but lukewarm and resting in the form of godliness. Give over your halting; be a true Christian; be zealous and repent; and then, though you have been an offence to Christ, you shall be the joy of His heart (Rev iii 16–20).

And now bear witness that mercy has been offered you. *'I call heaven and earth to record against you this day, that I have set before you life and death, blessing and cursing; therefore choose life, that you may live'* (Deut xxx 19). I can only entreat you and warn you. I cannot otherwise compel you to be happy; if I could, I would. What answer will you send me with to my Master? Let me speak to you as Abraham's servant to Nahor's family, *'And now if you will deal kindly and truly with my master, tell me.'* O for such a happy answer as Rebecca gave them: *'And they said, We will call the damsel, and inquire at her mouth. And they called Rebecca, and said unto her, Wilt thou go with this man? and she said, I will go'* (Gen xxiv 49–58). O that I had this from you! Why should I, who agonize for your salvation, be your accuser? Why should the passionate pleadings of mercy be turned into horrid aggravations of your obstinacy and additions to your misery? Judge in yourselves; do you not think their condemnation will be doubly dreadful, that shall still go on in their sins, after all endeavours to recall them? Doubtless it shall be more tolerable for Tyre and Sidon, yea, for Sodom and Gomorrah, in the day of judgment, than for you! (Mt xi 22–24).

Beloved, if you have any pity for your perishing souls, close with the present offers of mercy. If the God that made you have any authority with you, obey His command and come in. If you are not the despisers of grace, and would not shut the doors of mercy against yourselves, repent and be converted. Let not heaven stand open for you in vain. Let not the Lord Jesus open His stores and bid you buy without money and without price in vain. Let not His Spirit and His ministers strive with you in vain, and leave you now at last unpersuaded, lest the sentence go forth against you, *'The bellows are burned, the lead is consumed of the fire, the founder melteth in vain. Reprobate silver shall men call them, because the Lord hath rejected them'* (Jer vi 29–30).

'Father of spirits, take the heart in hand that is too hard for my weakness. Do not Thou end, though I have done. A word from Thy effectual power will do the work. O Thou, that hast the

key of David, that openest and no man shutteth, open Thou this heart, as Thou didst Lydia's, and let the King of Glory enter in, and make this soul Thy captive. Let not the tempter harden him in delays. Let him not stir from this place, nor take his eyes from these lines, till he resolve to forego his sins, and accept life on Thy self-denying terms. In Thy Name, O Lord God, did I go forth to these labours; in Thy name do I close them. Let not all the time they have cost be lost hours; let not all the thoughts of the heart, and all the pains that have been about them be lost labour. Lord, put Thy hand upon the heart of this reader, and send Thy Spirit, as once Thou didst Philip to join himself to the chariot of the eunuch while he was reading the Word. And though I should never know it while I live, yet I beseech Thee, O Lord God, let it be found at the last day that some souls are converted by these labours; and let some be able to stand forth and say that by these persuasions they were won unto Thee. Amen, Amen.' Let him that readeth say, Amen.